Sailing America
A Trailer Sailor's Guide
To North America

Sailing America
A Trailer Sailor's Guide to North America

LAWRENCE W. BROWN

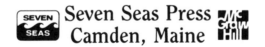 Seven Seas Press
Camden, Maine

Published by Seven Seas Press

10   9   8   7   6   5   4   3

Library of Congress Cataloging in Publication Data

Brown, Larry, 1946–
   Sailing America : a trailer sailor's guide to North America /
Lawrence W. Brown.
     p.   cm.
   ISBN 0-915160-96-X
   1. Sailing—North America—Guide-books. 2. North America—
Description and travel—1981—Guide-books. I. Title.
GV811.B716   1990
797.1'24'097—dc20
                                 90-30794
                                       CIP

Questions regarding the content of this book should be addressed to:

Seven Seas Press/International Marine Publishing
P.O. Box 220
Camden, ME 04843

Typeset by Camden Type 'n Graphics, Camden, ME
Printed by Arcata Graphics, Fairfield, PA
Design by Janet Patterson
Illustrated by the author
Production by Janet Robbins
Edited by Tom McCarthy, Jonathan Eaton
Photos by the author unless otherwise noted

To Bettina, Julie, and Amber, who have gone sailing America with me: My memories of the country are blended with my memories of you.

To all the makers of small boats, and to Joe Edwards in particular.

And to all the people who have offered their kindness: You have protected me not only from adversity, but from cynicism.

Contents

PART II
A Trailer Sailor's
Trip Guide
to North America

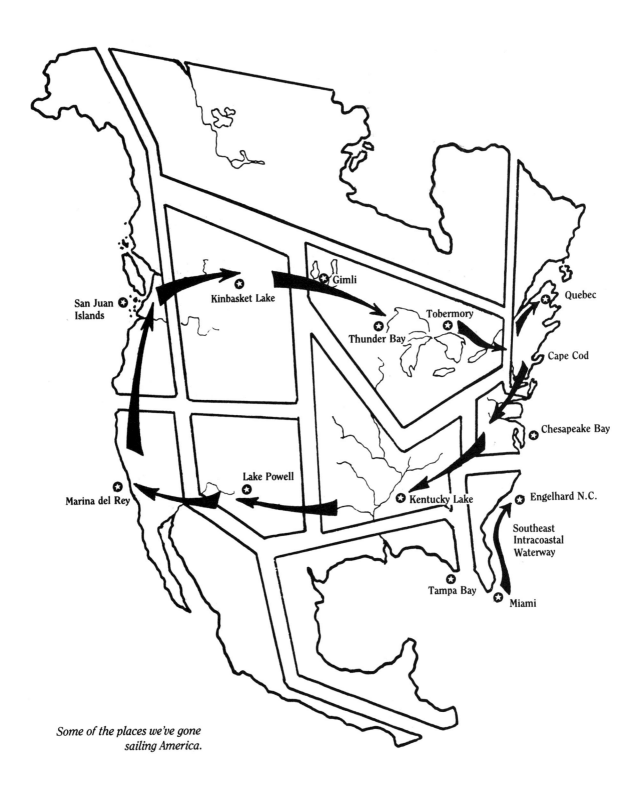

Some of the places we've gone sailing America.

PART

I

How to
Sail
America

CHAPTER 1

Introduction:
Discovering America
Under Sail

IT'S POSSIBLE, IF you're reading this, that you don't own a sailboat but wish you did. There you are, reading about someone's trip to Bora Bora and thinking, "Someday . . . someday I'm going to chuck it all and get me a big boat and just go." The sailing magazine settles to your lap; your eyes close and you see yourself bronzed and free at last—Bora Bora bound. A sailboat is one of the few powerful symbols of escape left to modern men and women.

Here's the rub. Ironically the problem with this fantasy is the main ingredient in its powerful appeal. To make it work, most of us would have to choose the fantasy over what we're currently doing. We'd have to give up a lot. Our *families* would have to really want to do this—passionately—or it wouldn't work either. Personally, I'm finding that my daughters, entering their teenage years, want stability more than anything else—a fixed point of reference while they, themselves, are changing so rapidly. It's happened more than once that a man, restless at his place in life, dreams of offering his family Bora Bora but they decline in favor of the old neighborhood. It's at around this point that he buys the family a 27- to 34-foot sailboat.

This boat, likely as not, will take its place among the rows and rows of floating monuments that crowd the nation's yachting harbors. Most of them just sit, making me wonder whether their owners want to *own* a boat more passionately than they want to go sailing in it. I doubt whether the new boats, many equipped with microwave ovens and VCRs, will actually encourage their owners to use them more. After all, the comforts of home are most conveniently enjoyed at home. Then too, when you sail out of your harbor on Saturday and come back on Sunday, you can only see so much.

My family and I, partially out of financial necessity, partially out of choice, went a radically different route. If we could not go to Bora Bora, we decided we *could* go to the Chesapeake Bay, the Tennessee Valley lakes, Lake Powell in Arizona, the Pacific at Los Angeles, the San Juan Islands in Washington, the Canadian Rocky lakes, Lake Winnipeg and Lake Manitoba, Thunder Bay on Superior, the North Channel of Huron, the St. Lawrence River. In New England we could sail on Lake Champlain, the Connecticut River out to Mystic Seaport, and our own Cape Cod. There was always Maine and the Hudson River to think about, and the Florida Keys and the long beautiful stretch of southern Atlantic coast. We could go sailing America. Some trips we did over a span of years, then one summer we covered 10,000 miles sailing as we went. We did all this with our family van and a 15-foot boat.

If you can't quit your job and chuck it all for global cruising, stay put; keep your family roots sunk down deep, and begin your adventure next summer. Get a portable sailboat; get out your road atlas and see what looks good to you. Here's the paradox of trailer sailing: The more modest your vessel, the more spectacular your travel possibilities. If the object is ownership, then a trailerable sailboat may seem unsatisfying and inadequate. If the object is *adventuring* (within the confines of your jobs and domestic schedules) there is no better way to do it. Less is more. What it takes is a completely fresh look at your approach to sailing. Here's how our own thinking went:

How to Go

If we were to go sailing America, we'd need to solve two very different kinds of problems. We'd need an automotive solution and a nautical solution: a caravan combination to sleep the whole family while motoring down the road, and a boat that would be easy to launch, seaworthy, and capable of sleeping everybody aboard. We solved the boat problem first. After years of sailing a West Wight Potter 15, we trusted the boat and felt we had learned how to cruise in a boat that small. Filler boards and a boomtent could convert the cockpit into a second cabin for our daughters, if need be. We also carried a pup tent for camping ashore. Monkey hammocks and knapsacks hung from the cabin walls would keep our clothes off the bunks. We knew it worked.

A further thought: A boat with four bunks would be not only bulkier to haul around, it also would create a routine in which we spent all day together in the car and then all night together in a small boat. While family togetherness is an admirable goal, there is a point of excess. At least along generational lines, some provision for separation and privacy made sense. This thinking suggested the ideal motor vehicle: a minivan, convertible into a dormitory for our two daughters. Then, on the road, our girls would have the van with its lights, lockable doors, and stereo— we would have the boat.

The West Wight Potter people consented to using this trip as an engineering experiment. I wanted to try out a shoal-keel design, sacrificing the extremely easy launching and beaching abilities of the traditional centerboard boat for a gain in interior space, including a full unobstructed double berth. My design modification was built with deep misgivings on their part, understandable after 27 years of continuous

Fearless was an experimental shoal-keel Potter 15, giving me an opportunity to rearrange the interior. We had an unobstructed double berth and a footwell in lieu of a centerboard. There was surprising room.

production, but they were curious, too. For our part, we were Potter enthusiasts of long standing, but we needed just a *little* more room . . . and we got it with *Fearless*. Happiness all around.

To haul ourselves and our boat, we purchased a Toyota minivan. I've never been crazy about the station wagon approach to seating, where the whole bed platform is either made or unmade. On a long haul, one passenger might wish to sleep and one to sit, so we got a cargo van and not only saved a lot of money but installed our own interior. The back seats recline or sit up individually, and they are mounted on a carpeted platform raised a foot off the van floor, permitting storage underneath. The seats—foam-block chairs from a discount store—can be laid out perfectly flat, providing a luxurious mattress 7 inches thick for sleeping. The van, as we hoped, ran through 10,000 complaint-free miles, up mountains, through deserts. The boat and van combo was a marriage made in heaven.

Caravanning

Though your primary goal may be sailing, you should, if you're planning an expedition of this sort, get used to thinking of your car and your boat as a unit—a "caravan" on the highway. In it, you'll have beds, at least one toilet (we had two), cooking gear, and storage. You can be independent of hotels and even campgrounds if you want or need to be. Actually, if your experience matches ours, you'll find campgrounds with sites available almost everywhere—especially on weekdays. They're your best bet. You'll have showers, laundries, and often pools and congenial neighbors. If you're traveling with kids, they'll find other kids and get some respite from each other's constant company, all for an easy price.

We often found ourselves getting tired along the route and would simply look for a place to pull over. Places of choice: service islands along throughways, state information center parking lots, and designated picnic or rest areas. We learned to avoid truck parking areas, as the truckers often leave their motors (or generators) running all night long, and often rumble off loudly at 2 or 3 o'clock in the morning. We avoided totally unprotected or isolated areas, but despite the random horror story one hears, in 48 days on the road we often left our car unlocked—and the windows open—and experienced no vandalism, no theft.

Once, in Manitoba, I had driven late into the night and stopped in a roadside diner for coffee. Tired and a bit spaced, I paid my bill and left my wallet on the counter. When I returned to my van, I turned on the lights and started an entry in my journal. After a while, a boy startled me, tapping on my window. "Are you Lawrence Brown?" he asked. "I'm glad we caught you; we've been calling every motel in the area." He handed me my wallet.

Karl Malden is right: you should carry traveler's checks, but be prepared also for honesty. Finding unexpected virtue is one of the great satisfactions of travel.

Some nights, heat or pounding rain and wind will make camping impractical. Plan on spending one night of every four in a motel; budget for it. Especially if you have kids and if you're going to be on the road more than a week, it'll be a real tonic.

Finally, if you're planning an inland sailing expedition, equip your car and your boat with screens. After sailing on Kentucky Lake, I drove late into the night while the kids slept. Only after the lights of an all-night gas station played into the interior of our van did I see the cloud of mosquitoes, sucked in over the miles through my open windows, hovering over my children. In the suddenly still air, they discovered me and swarmed forward. I made a beeline, swatting and cursing, to the nearest motel. These aren't sea tales, but I tell them to make a point: When you go trailer sailing, caravanning your boat down the highway, you should come away with land tales too. You will, after all, cover more miles on the highways than you will under sail. Relish those miles. Check your car and your whole rig in a seamanlike way. (Vibration is your greatest enemy.) Make wide turns; be conservative in every move you make—as you would under sail. Then open your senses to take in fully every mile you travel, being reminded by the boat you see following you in the mirror that you're doing something very out of the ordinary. We found *no one* doing what we were doing, and I'm convinced that there are far more people circumnavigating the globe under sail than there are circumnavigating America with a boat in tow. That's ironic, since most people can't really pull up stakes and go sailing around the planet, but almost anyone can do what we've been doing—in smaller increments if not all at once.

Sailing America: One Family's Experience

We left Cape Cod on the 20th of June and headed south for Chesapeake Bay. The Chesapeake had multiple appeals: a clan of cousins I love and rarely get to see, a host of memories from my first sailing experiences on family boats, and the area itself, which features charm, an easy pace, good sailing, and good eating. Our favorite spot has always been Oxford, on Maryland's tranquil Eastern Shore. So after a brief stopover with family in Philadelphia, we headed right for it.

The town of Oxford possesses a long history running back past Revolutionary War days. Its brick sidewalks and old buildings haven't changed much, probably. Oxford has a comfortable, lived-in feeling that suggests residents who love the life they live and go on about their business largely for the joy of it, rather than to impress anyone. If that approach is colonial, I'm all for it.

The region is a sailor's paradise, but it's not interested in becoming a sailor's Mecca. Oxford isn't set up to attract hordes of yachting pilgrims. The town's several excellent yards principally take care of their own, and nicely accommodate the occasional visitor who motors in. We launched *Fearless* at the town ramp on Tilghman Street, then motored back to visit Applegarth's Marine Yard, builder of at least 40 wooden skipjacks over the years.

Applegarth's is nestled back behind the town. It's a colorful nest of old wooden structures and timeworn docks. As the Chesapeake tides are more moderate than in New England, the docks have a relaxed, low-slung feeling to them. Yard manager Bob Bavernfeind emerged shirtless from under a boat to chat.

Upon the recent death of the senior Applegarth, a builder was waiting to pounce on the property to erect condominiums, but the town rose up and blocked the move. Bob hoped the yard could hang on being itself and doing its traditional thing. As he spoke, he smoothed a new centerboard trunk in a wooden daysailer. "Fellow in Ohio owns this. So much rot in her, he leaves it with me every winter to work on."

Outdoors, an overcast was burning off, and sunlight streamed in through cracks in the planked walls and through the open end of the shed. Inside, however, the light was muted, vaguely conjuring the nave of a church. A dishevelled church it would be, though, with coils of line hanging on the walls, piles of wood, a skipjack rudder leaning against something indistinct in the shadows: If you're looking for the old-time religion, you'll find it here, or at Cutts & Case, or almost anywhere nearby. Here they still believe in wooden boats.

Just for fun, I pulled up next to a 16-foot skipjack—a tiny replica of the beamy, traditional workboats. It was a faithful replica, right down to its kerosene running lights board-mounted to the shrouds. Its white canvas sails were snugged down to the bowsprit and nestled in lazyjacks along the boom. The owner had the transom partially torn out and was replacing sections of it with freshly cut wood.

Below, the boat had a familiar layout: two bunks ran along the centerboard. I snuggled in and just fit. "Oh you can sleep in her, all right," the owner sang out. "There's lots of room." And so there was. Not a tiny boatlength away was another miniature skipjack just like it. I like to think my Potter has become, in the age of fiberglass, a little classic, but these fellows have me beat. The little skipjacks could just as easily have been built a hundred years ago.

That's a large part of the charm of the Eastern Shore. Much of it *was* built a hundred years ago, if not two or three. The weather turned and, in a fine drizzle, I putted around for a while, nosed out into the Choptank River (great sailing), and then pulled *Fearless* back out. That night, cousin May and I feasted on soft-shell Maryland crabs. I remembered

At Applegarth's Marina in Oxford, Maryland, Fearless *nestles next to a 16-foot micro-cruiser from a half century ago—a miniature skipjack.*

sailing on our Tahiti ketch when I was a boy, hanging off the bowsprit with a crabnet. My brother and I would compete to see who could snatch up the most crabs as they sunned themselves on the surface of the water. Traditions run in families as well as in regions.

Someone joined our conversation. "Have you been to St. Michaels? It's all changed. We don't want that here. We'll keep it the same, if we can."

SOUTH BY WEST

Touring the nation's capital with a boat in tow was hot and tedious business. Traffic was heavy and facilities at hand did not appear to permit parking a boat and trailer anywhere. We were confined, therefore, to a passing view of points of interest from our windows. I had wanted to take a memorable shot of the boat and trailer against some imposing backdrop such as the Washington Monument, but the press of traffic made that impossible. The girls said afterward they'd rather have taken Interstate 495 around the city and made tracks west. To my surprise, I agreed with them. The mountains of Virginia drew more response from all of us.

After a quick jaunt on Route 66, we were running on Route 81 down along the Shenandoah River, at one point crossing over it. What a sight the Shenandoah made running a placid course through a chasm of eroded rock. There would be a river trip worth taking!

We ended up at a campground just south of Woodstock, Virginia. Campgrounds and other facilities are generously marked along highways and we had a choice of locations, none of them crowded.

This was our first night away from the bosom of family and relatives, our first night sleeping two plus two. The arrangement was basically sound. One thing I noticed is that movement in the van is magnified through the tongue of the trailer, and it was annoying being rocked around every time one of the girls rolled over in bed. Whenever practical, it's a good idea to disconnect the two, brace the boat so you can move around on it, and be a bit more separate. With younger children, maybe additional peace of mind could be had living with the jostle of being connected, just to have a better feel what was going on in there. Oddly enough, movement in the boat does not have a similar effect on the van. Maybe that's just as well.

The Virginia countryside was a welcome relief from the heat and congestion of Washington, D.C. While the glimpses we got of the Shenandoah were enticing, we found, on inquiry, that it is more a canoeist's than a sailor's paradise. One could put in on the lower Shenandoah and head down into the Potomac, then down past Washington D.C., there maybe to tie up and tour the city by guide bus before continuing down to the Chesapeake.

The southwestern trek from Woodstock into West Virginia is rougher going for a trailered boat, even a Potter, with one lane each way and tedious mountain roads. I couldn't risk the distraction of a glance at much of the scenery. Gradually the switchbacks evened out, the country began to open up, and we found ourselves running down along the New River gorge. A series of dams creates obstacles along the river, but the lower sections would be a very different excursion for anyone willing to drive it. West Virginia isn't "Dawgpatch" anymore, but the New River boasts an unusual texture of wilderness, smoking industry, and an incongruous assortment of housing arrangements. The effect is oddly harmonious. The lower end of the river is a national park. Route 60 continues to Huntington, where we crossed the Ohio River in the early evening. The sun set downriver and, as we traversed the bridge, a paddlewheeler passed under us. I strained my ears to hear Dixieland over the sound of the traffic. Clearly we were getting south.

The next really alluring sailing grounds were the Kentucky Lakes. Tennessee and Kentucky both have a generous sprinkling of lakes, but the crown jewels have got to be the twin Tennessee Valley Authority lakes, Barkley and Kentucky. We dipped south off the Bluegrass Parkway onto Route 65 and visited Mammoth Cave along the way. As you near the national park, local entrepreneurs lure you off the path with look-alike signs: Mammoth Onyx Cave . . . Mammoth Mushroom Cave . . . etc. Tired and buzzed from the heat, we pulled off into an amusement park, lured by one of the signs that shouted "Cave Entrance," in large letters. The rides distracted the kids for a while—time we all agreed later would have been better spent at the national park.

Not only is Mammoth Cave enormous, with more than 309 charted underground miles of cave, it is fascinating, otherworldly and, best of all on a summer day, a wonderful refuge from the heat. We would have taken several tours had enough of the day been left. We ended the day on a waterslide, ate at Ma & Pa's restaurant, and crashed at an inexpensive motel just up the road.

The two TVA lakes are beautiful, unspoiled, and well-equipped with ramps and campgrounds. We chose the larger of the two, Kentucky Lake, which straddles the Kentucky-Tennessee border. With 160,000 acres of water and 2,380 miles of shoreline, this is the largest man-made lake system in the country. Showing up in the middle of a heatwave, we still had no trouble finding a campsite on the water from where we could pull

There's some beautiful but demanding country in West Virginia if you're pulling a boat.

*Kentucky Lake and Lake Barkley
are serene and pastoral.*

Fearless around to the beach. This area is capable of absorbing a huge number of tourists and campers without packing them in like sardines.

It was our misfortune to visit for two breathless days under a broiling summer sun. I'm told the sailing is good there, with useful east and southwest winds. We'll take it on faith. You easily could spend a week or two, get in some good sailing, some comfortable swimming, and completely unwind. This is not a vacation that would stretch the capabilities of a seasoned sailor. It would be an ideal location for a beginning sailing family, or a reminder for oceangoing types that the enjoyment of sailing doesn't always hinge on a feeling of having prevailed, or survived, against the elements. The elements are pretty benign in southwestern Kentucky.

Many people wouldn't think of buying a car without air conditioning. We acquired our car late, and because it was a cargo van, it was not equipped with air conditioning. We ordered a white van to minimize solar heating of the interior, and installed a ceiling hatch all the way aft to attone for a lack of opening side windows anywhere except the front doors. Opened, the hatch admitted a nice flow of air through the car; removed, it induced a veritable blast of through-flowing ventilation. For a northern trip and for summer driving in our home area of New England, these provisions would have been sufficient. For southern travel especially, but for long trips in general, I'm now convinced that air conditioning is not a luxury; it's a necessity.

First of all and obviously, air conditioning beats the heat. A heavy draft of 100-degree air flowing through the car beats *no* draft, but a full day of that is a wilting and dehydrating punishment. Then there's noise. When you travel with all the windows down, you're buffeted by not only heat and wind but by sound. Trucks thunder and whine by, blanketing conversation. You can't hear the radio, or by the time it's turned up loud enough for the kids in back, you can't stand it up front. Conversations between the seats are slowly reduced to brief exchanges of calls and shouts. Our kids were troupers, but several days of this took their toll. Squabbles became more frequent and more heartfelt. At the end of the day we felt battered. If you can afford it, get air conditioning when you get the car. It will tax the engine and reduce your mileage, but the car is made of steel and you and your family are not. It will transform your trip.

Arkansas was a swelter of heat made more unendurable at night by swarms of tiny mosquitoes that bit hard and clung to our skin like cobwebs whenever we ventured outside. They even clung one night to our motel door and flooded in as we entered the room. Thoughtfully, the establishment had provided each room with a fly swatter.

The next morning the van was infested with them hiding under seats, in shoes, under boxes and blankets, behind curtains. Once roused, they headed unerringly for me, so I alternated banging around in the already sweltering van, rousting them out, and darting back out onto the tarmac dancing and swatting them away after they had transferred their allegiance to me. It took several forays to de-bug the van. Needless to say, such an area could be unmitigated hell for campers if their screens were inadequate or if they were forced to choose between stifling in their van or boat, the screens blocking what light breeze there might be, or venturing outdoors to the grateful horde of mosquitoes.

In Oklahoma, the terrain began to feel less southern than western. In western Oklahoma, a wonderful thing happened: A wave of unseasonably cool air flooded in and we dropped down into New Mexico in comfort. Almost instantly, the scenery turned spectacular, combining huge expanses of sky with flat-topped buttes and impressive rock formations. Now *this* was the real West we had come to see!

New Mexico's terrain changes frequently, with fascinating abruptness. Some state auto licenses are not to be believed. "You've got a friend in Pennsylvania," one reads. Oh, sure. But New Mexico's says "Land of Enchantment," and that's, if anything, an understatement.

If there's any complaint with New Mexico, it's the state's tolerance of billboards. "Seven miles to the Dairy Queen," or some such thing, a cluster of three more spaced a hundred yards apart, then more later, then a final orgy of signs as we neared the site—almost a dozen in all. It was a shame to see such country, basically untouched by the hand of man, defaced in such a trivial way.

It's a good idea when traveling in the desert to keep your gas tank fairly full, and to carry plenty to drink. There are occasional gaps in service—such as a 60-mile stretch from Albuquerque, New Mexico, south to Casa Blanca. Some small stations close at 5 or 6 o'clock. If you're driving windows down, dehydration can make you tired and listless, disinclined even to open a can of soda. Keep the flow of fluids going with emergency water. Bring several extra gallons—to drink, for boilover, or breakdown.

The heat returned in Arizona, and the scenery dutifully changed again—flatter and more barren. We passed what looked like furnace-scorched outcroppings of rock. In these black canyons, a traveler on foot would literally be baked to a crisp.

Arizona's big surprise is the scenery around Jerome and Prescott. Heading southwest toward Phoenix things gradually become alpine. Then there are lawns, trees, and pastureland. The heat relents. Farther on, deep

Julie takes the plunge.

canyons open up. We passed the Salt River Canyon and paused repeatedly to take in the view. It was tedious going, towing a boat, but the scenery justified the effort. Then down, down, into heat and, at last, the varieties of cactus one associates with desert country. We stopped at the house of some dear friends; the kids piled out of the car, relieved to find space and company of other youngsters. The longest and hardest stretch of driving was behind us.

LAKE POWELL

As we drove north from Phoenix, the heat slowly eased with altitude until we found ourselves putting on extra gear. We arrived at the Arizona end of Lake Powell in the dark—without a clue, aside from brochure and magazine pictures, of how the place looked. Sunrise blew our minds. A high table desert stretches away in all directions, dotted here and there by buttes and huge rock formations that rise abruptly from the ground. The pastels change continually as the sun makes its tour of the heavens.

The lake itself reaches nearly 100 miles into Utah, lacing itself around rock formations, running back into canyons. The most enthusiastic travel brochure you can lay your hands on will not have overstated its case. This is a fantasy land—a quality not lost on filmmakers over the years who have chosen this area for biblical epics, westerns, and science fiction movies such as *Planet of the Apes.*

We approached the lake from the south on Route 89, crossed the bridge that overlooks Glen Canyon Dam, and camped at the Wahweap area. The camping and boating facilities there are the best on the lake, the best we saw *anywhere* in fact. The launch ramp easily could handle seven boats at a time, and a second ramp a mile or two away boasted eight lanes. We woke up with our first flat trailer tire, and the gas station at the ramps mended it in 10 minutes. A restaurant, store, and laundromat are all within an easy walk; a mammoth parking lot absorbs cars and trailers.

Such facilities are more than a luxury; they're a necessity. This lake is *heavily* used on weekends, almost exclusively by powerboats. As we drove up Sunday night, the cars streamed southward to Phoenix, every third one, it seemed, towing a motorboat of some kind. On the lake itself, houseboats seemed the thing to have—floating apartments with porches and decks from which to admire the scenery.

While I'm a romantic and a devotee of sail, this lake makes its own case for powerboating. It's a long, long lake with narrow passes and hundreds of deep, winding canyons. From Wahweap, Rainbow Bridge is a several hours' drive by fast boat. People there seem to use the lake like a highway, cruising from place to place at top speed, admiring the view as it flies by. Ours was the only sailboat we saw on the lake or on the road to and from during our whole time there.

For sailors, this is a lake to savor in detail. Because of the uncanny clarity of the air, things seem closer than they are, over land or water. The fun for us was less in the "passagemaking" than the exploration of canyons, just drinking in the views as they unfolded. We did our share of climbing and walking. We camped for the night in a deep canyon with a sandy beach created from the wind-scoured sandstone back wall. When a motorboat showed up our initial reaction was irritation at the loss of our privacy, but our guests proved cordial and we were soon grateful for the friendship. They showed the girls a rock wall with hand grips carved into it and, to my horror and admiration, Amber and Julie began scaling 20 feet up the cliff and jumping off into the deep water below.

The swimming in Powell is unsurpassed. The water is a clean emerald green when you're on it; it's cool and refreshing yet you can stay in it for hours without getting the chills. Beware of the sun though. This is a place for longsleeved white shirts and pants and a good hat. The sun at midday will fry you for lunch while you're having too good a time to notice. If you're hot with your clothes on, jump in and let evaporative cooling refresh you for a half hour or so. Good sunblocks and soothing lotions are a must.

If you plan to camp ashore or beach your boat overnight, good screens and some bug repellent are in order. We found no mosquitoes but zillions of gnats that swarmed out of the sand and rocks after dark. When the sun returned, they found new hiding places in our clothes, our shoes, the folds of the sail, partially finished drink boxes, everywhere. A thorough banging around sent up clouds of the little rascals. They didn't bite much, though—just made you itch when they landed. Light attracts them by the thousands. Don't read after dark unless your screening is perfect.

With all deference to the places we had visited, Powell was the most captivating to date, though a houseboater from Utah spoke in equally awestruck tones of Cape Cod, our home base.

THE PACIFIC

We left Lake Powell and headed for Los Angeles by way of the Grand Canyon. My daughters, after all their travels, still consider Vermont their favorite place on the planet, and so, to my amazement, they found the canyon more depressing than awesome. It epitomized, to them, the aridity and monumental inhospitality of the desert. It gave them the willies. "Let's get out of here," Julie said.

Certain parts of the country seem reflective of a mood or an emotion, while other places, such as the great Southwest, seem to be the expression of some enormous divine thought—a huge, ungraspable *Idea*. The colossal buttes and mesas with their table-flat tops do more than diminish the traveler in his car, crawling across the desert at their feet. They suggest a strangeness, an *otherness* not felt in other places. "Your ways are not my ways," God says to Job. "Neither are your thoughts my thoughts." I have a hunch that the Pueblo and Navajo Indians, living on that particular land, know something cosmic the rest of us probably don't.

We left Arizona and smoldered down through an awful part of the desert so infernal that even the resourceful Indians appear to have rejected it, to Needles, California: 114 degrees in the shade at 9 o'clock that night. We collapsed at our Aunt Judy's place in Palm Desert for a day, then headed west to the Pacific.

If New York is the Big Apple, is L.A. the Big Orange? We drove past acres of windmills—huge "windfarms"—then through cropland blending quickly into suburb. The approach to L.A. seems interminable; it's pleasant but uniform, mile after mile of the same thing under a beige-blue sky. "Will we ever get there?" the kids kept asking. We had covered four thousand miles.

In L.A., we were the guests of the West Wight Potter people and they generously put us up in style at the Marina del Rey Hotel. The comforts of home have nothing on Marina del Rey: Here was a pool, TV, Disneyland, Universal Studios, all sorts of places to eat. For me, there was the Pacific.

The California coast differs from the New England coast in one fundamental way: Whereas the latter is convoluted and blessed with hundreds of shelters and harbors, the Pacific coast is bold and unprotected for stretches of 40 to 50 miles or more. Catalina Island makes a nice 26-mile offshore passage, but most of the time, sailors out of L.A. must either commit to a trip of some consequence or opt instead for daysailing.

The town of Marina del Rey boasts launching and storage facilities second to none. The town has storage for *hundreds* of trailered boats, space for another hundred or so empty trailers, and, of course, the huge Marina del Rey itself. You can feast your eyes on thousands of beautiful, unused boats baking in the sun day after day. Joe Edwards, president of HMS Marine, wanted to try out the shoal-keel Potter, so he launched and rigged the boat and we enjoyed a sail together in the harbor. Later, I went out into the Pacific on my own. A heavy stone breakwater guarded the entrance to the harbor, and beyond that stretched the wide Pacific.

As I neared the breakwater, the ocean breeze grew stronger. There were good swells running too. This was fun: bounding along the edge of an ocean that encircles half the world. Who should I find out there but another chap in a Potter 15. We hailed one another, then began a conversation at the top of our lungs as we surfed down the crests of the waves. It was a high moment. Finally I headed back in and he turned out to sea. "Where are you going?" I yelled. "A few miles out," he called back, "heave to and spend the night. Do it all the time." He yelled something more but I couldn't get it all—just the last line: "I love it!"

There's an abruptness to sailing in the Pacific from Marina del Rey. You slip out past a breakwater and you're in it—without another harbor for 50 miles.

The next day I had my first chance to do some ocean sailing in a Potter 19. The wind was about the same; the waves were even more majestic. It was a beautiful day, and despite my long affection for *Fearless*, I found myself thinking impure thoughts about what I could do with a bigger boat. Meanwhile, back at the plant, an experimental trailer built by Kross Kountry arrived. Designed by Norm Reynolds, it was built specifically to sling the shoal-keel as low to the highway as possible. From that point on, we could approximate, though not duplicate, the launching ease of the standard boat. The HMS factory crew assembled the new trailer for us and helped wrestle *Fearless* onto it. Then we said our good-byes and many thank-yous and having gone as far west as we could go, turned north.

NORTH BY NORTHWEST

Our next objective was the San Juan Islands nestled between Vancouver Island and Washington. By one of those wonderful coincidences, we had been invited to visit the San Juans by a couple we had never met before. Bill and Betty-Lou McKinney sell Potters and run a charter operation in the Seattle-Portland area. Planning the trip, no sooner had I added the San Juans to the itinerary than an invitation from Bill arrived.

The coastal drive north from L.A. along the Pacific is one of the most breathtaking anywhere in the world. Being northbound puts you on the *inside* edge rather than the cliffside edge of the road, and with a boat in tow, that's more comforting.

Monterey would be a beautiful cruising-exploring area for a small-boat sailor, and the town is picturesque with much to do and see. Farther north, San Francisco Bay is a spectacular cruising ground provided you've had the foresight to sew one or two good sets of reef points in your mainsail. More northerly still and about 80 miles inland from Eureka, is the Mount Shasta Lake region, with snowcapped Shasta providing a beautiful backdrop for the several lakes you might visit. California—from the Baja to Shasta—would host an ideal vacation in and of itself. Maybe no other state in the Union combines so many extremes and offers such variety and intensity of experience.

We followed a trail of mountains into Washington and then, north of Seattle, boarded a ferry out to the San Juans. We ferried our whole caravan to Lopez Island and drove off into an idyllic pastoral setting. The air was cool, our surroundings lush and green. Suddenly the desert seemed far away. A line of snowcapped peaks rimmed part of the horizon.

The McKinneys instantly fell in love with our girls (and our girls with them), and they said a wonderful thing to us: "Amber and Julie will be just fine; why don't you kids take off in the boat and have some time by yourselves?" The girls, too, thought that a splendid idea, and so we were all agreed.

The San Juan Islands experience tremendous tides, so launch ramps are useful only at specific times. Because of these tides and currents, the Pacific boils through the islands with unusual vigor, producing modest whirlpools and strange localized flows. Meanwhile, the winds may be light. Without a dependable motor, you might think you're in a vast Disneyland ride—drifting backward and sideways through the scenery. Our Eska 2 motor proved easily up to that; it doesn't take much to drive a 500-pound boat.

This is a beautiful cruising ground occupied by unusually gracious people, but it's perhaps not an ideal place for the uninitiated unless you've got someone like Bill McKinney for a guide. The water is cold, 45 degrees,

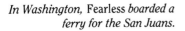

In Washington, Fearless *boarded a ferry for the San Juans.*

and if you sail or drift outside the protection of the islands, you enter some of the most treacherous waters in the Northwest. The islands, while beautiful, look much alike, and one could grow easily confused. It is an area to savor with respect.

Lopez Island seemed at first to be a teacher's colony. The McKinneys and most of the people we met there were teachers. Their jobs leave their summers free, and their temperaments blend perfectly with the feeling of the island itself. If the waters around the island command vigilance, the land does not. There the unsettling influences of the 20th century are a dimly felt memory. Our kids could wander anywhere they liked day or night without anyone's concern. Our first night on the island, neighbors along the little dirt road gathered at the beach for a cookout, and we all felt the collective warmth and tolerance extend itself to us as if we were visiting family. Later on, the family of a beachfront house made ready to raise a lofty TV antenna, and half the neighborhood swarmed up ladders to help out while the other half nursed their beers on the ground and sent up a continuous stream of humor and advice. My wife and I found ourselves speculating about how we might arrange to live out there.

By the second and third day on Lopez, we began to appreciate a second quality of life in a teacher colony: There was a refreshing current of intellectual and artistic awareness. It wasn't there to impress anyone; it was simply a byproduct of assembling a critical mass of literate people in one place. The favorite eating and drinking spot enjoyed a steady flow of visiting jazz musicians, who often played for free.

An agreeable sail took us past an island with a French-speaking summer camp to Friday Harbor on Orcas Island. We visited an excellent museum devoted to the misnamed "killer" whales and had a good lunch, but we already missed the easy pace and lack of pretense we found on Lopez. A seal popped his nose and beady eyes out of the water on our return, then huffed and sank out of sight. We came back on a sunset, purple water, and a gentle wind.

From the San Juans, it was a relatively short ride into Canada and Vancouver. Canadian customs was, as always in our experience, cordial and helpful, offering us advice and suggestions on routes and things to see. By nightfall, we were following the Fraser River into the Canadian Rockies. As we did, we turned the corner on our expedition and, for the first time, headed ourselves back east.

HIGHWATER SAILING

As you enter the Rockies from Vancouver, you pick up the Trans-Canada Highway, which you can ride all the way across the country. It's a modest road by United States standards, but it's a beautiful one. American interstates have a numbing sameness at times that dulls your sense of having actually traveled through the country to any place different. In Canada, the road has *texture*. Moreover, we found ourselves rounding each bend in the highway to a mountain vista more spectacular than the last. Finally we confronted a phalanx of snowcapped gray giants so breathtaking I bailed out of the car and shot half a roll of film before Bettina wrestled me to the ground and made me get a grip on myself.

Then the McKinneys said a wonderful thing to us: "Why don't you and Bettina take off for some time by yourselves and leave the kids with us."

I had long suspected Powell and the Rockies would be our most spectacular places to visit and I was itching to get *Fearless* into one of those lakes I had seen on postcards all my life. I learned something quickly: Many of the postcard lakes are *very* small—reflecting pools for the view. Launching into one would be like putting into the reflecting pool of the Washington Monument just for the sake of some spectacular pictures. Then too, the park commissions don't permit anything bigger than a canoe in many of the lakes.

Fortunately there are several really large lakes, any one of which would be worthy of a vacation in itself.

Shuswap Lake runs for miles and miles along the Trans-Canada in west-central British Columbia. It's enormous, scenic, and open to boats of all types. As a bonus, the water there is warm, at least by mountain standards.

We chose instead to put in on Kinbasket Lake a bit farther northwest. Attracted by a sign advertising "Big Lake Resort," we followed a logging road down an endless chain of switchbacks until we ended up at a rustic campground on a bluff overlooking the lake. Snowcapped mountains were a distant backdrop everywhere we looked. Best of all, there was a continuous breeze. Against all odds, the Rockies are a sailor's paradise. The wind is *always* blowing on the lake—either up or down. Had we time, we could have explored a hundred miles uplake into the back country. (Hell, *every*where up there is "back country.") There are bears in the woods, black and grizzly, pack rats big as small dogs, and if they don't get you, there are clouds of mosquitoes waiting to carry you off. The lake, though, with its breeze, was bugfree and full of fish. After tucking in a double reef, we set out in whitecaps and had a rousing sail.

Soon we found ourselves dodging floating logs and fantastically patterned tangles of driftwood, products of the intensive logging around the lake. For us it was more nuisance than hazard, but a speedboat soon would have torn out its bottom—but there were no speedboats. The resort dock had a few boats tied up that people used for fishing, but basically, we were the only boat on the entire lake. Had we pressed northward for a day or so, we probably would not have seen a single human being.

Left: motoring into the Rockies. Right: a look up Kinbasket to the Narrows, Bettina at the helm.

On one level, not seeing anybody would have been a shame, because at the camp we met some generous and fascinating folks. Whatever they lacked in scholarship they more than made up in grit and humor. For many of them, wilderness living was a deliberate year-round choice. Several men there were truckers who drove the ice roads north in the winter. One driver, over a shared dinner, explained: "The rivers and creeks freeze up near solid in the winter, and they make flat, open paths through the woods and mountains. You have to drive those to take stuff in and out to the logging and mining camps up there. Of course the ice cracks some. You know you're all right when you can hear it making a cracking, splitting noise. Scares the hell out of you at first but you're all right. When it makes a high squealing sound, then you know you're in for it. Then you stomp on it and barrel past as fast as you can so you don't fall through. It's at least 50 below up there. Fall through and you're dead. Even if you have a radio it won't do no good—you'll be just as dead when they find you, but they'll start looking quicker."

I wondered if they got hazardous-duty pay. "Special pay, shit," he said. "It's just pay, it's a job. Besides, I really like it here. It's a good place for my wife and kids and," he grinned, "the fishing's good."

When rain shut down the sailing, we hit the road and drove up to see the Athabasca Glacier. These glaciers—there are several in the Rockies—are ice ages in miniature. Containing keys to our past and possibly to our future, they bear watching. The Canadian government has specialists keeping an eye on this one, lest it take it into its head to go south and grind the Dakotas. In its present quiescent state, the Athabasca Glacier is a thousand feet thick, so heavy it grinds the rock on which it sits into a powder of talcum fineness. This rock flour, flowing with the meltwater, colors the glacial lakes and streams a pale jade green. Kinbasket had it. Cup your hands and dip into a rivulet melting off the glacier's face and sip water locked into ice when the pyramids were built. Tastes good.

In southwestern Alberta east of Banff, as you leave the Rockies, is the last of the really spectacular lakes: Lake Minnewanka. Rimmed with snowcapped mountains, it's open to boats of all kinds, so if Kinbasket seems too remote for comfort, here you might at least see *somebody* on the water.

The highway east drops out of the mountains with amazing abruptness. Behind you the Rockies run north and south like a granite curtain; before you, the vast central plains of Canada stretch out for 2,000 miles. Suddenly it's flat, and the Rockies seem like something you dreamed of but no one has actually ever seen.

We had been on the road 38 days. Bettina's job at *The Cape Cod Times* required her return, and the girls were exhausted. They had, by then, seen everything they had wanted to see originally and long surpassed their tolerance for continuous travel. So they joined Bettina on the plane and from Calgary flew home to Cape Cod. Suddenly I had the whole caravan to myself—a choice of beds. The prospect was depressing. Their plane lifted off into a morning so clear I could count the individual snowy peaks of the Rockies 110 miles away. I felt solitary and unhappy without everybody's company, but the prairie was beautiful in its way and soon cheered me up. Being alone with my thoughts, I rediscovered and cultivated the resources of my own company. If the main part of the trip was a rare chance to commune with my kids, the last leg of it was an equally rare chance to commune with myself.

If you decide to go traveling with your kids, be aware of their need for continuity, for a home base. Occupants of larger motor homes sometimes turn them into self-contained space capsules and roll through America observing the country through the neutralizing glass of their own windows. Any chance to stay put for a while will bring welcome stability to your children. To the extent they become familiar with a place, they can wander off safely and decompress away from the enforced intimacy of car and boat.

By the end of the trip I also learned that my kids resisted adult enthusiasm over scenic vistas and such. The electronic media have conditioned them to a higher level of stimulation. Still, I learned they are taking in far more than we think they are. The adult mistake is expecting things to mean the same to our kids that they mean to us. Things won't. Julie and Amber were turned off by Washington D.C., but, on the same day, enchanted by the Virginia scenery, which reminded them of Vermont. It's good to be patient with kids. It may take them six months or more to digest a meal as big as North America.

TO THE GREAT LAKES

Lakes Manitoba and Winnipeg lie in western Manitoba to the northwest of the Great Lake system, but they are, by almost any standard, great lakes themselves. Lake Manitoba, the less developed of the two, stretches more than a hundred miles into the north country and is more than thirty miles across at its widest. With an average depth of only 14 feet, Manitoba could become a vile body of water in foul weather, and a sailor in trouble would be a long way from organized assistance. The same could be said of Lake Winnipegosis, a narrower, even longer lake nestled near Manitoba's northwest shoreline. On the positive side, these are beautiful prairie lakes. The wind blows all the time up there, and with a well-found, shallow-draft boat you could do some spectacular wilderness sailing. Best of all, the water can reach a comfortable 70 degrees in summer. Swimming is great!

Lake Winnipeg is, by far, the most massive lake in the prairie lake system. It's almost two lakes, pinched nearly in two by a narrows 75 miles from the southern shore. The lower lake, up to 45 miles across, is sandy, much deeper than Manitoba, and more settled. The upper lake is more rocky, clearer, and colder. One could put in, as I did, at Winnipeg Beach on the western shore and sail, as I did not, 150 miles north. Winnipeg is easily a whole vacation's worth of lake.

I sailed from a delightful little harbor into the biggest rollers I'd seen since the Pacific. As the wind mounted with the rising sun, I practiced "fire drills" with *Fearless.* I hove-to with just the jib and tied in a reef, then I tried working to windward with various combinations of reefs, with and without the jib, heaving-to between each maneuver to think about things. The morning was capped by a rousing downwind run, surfing the waves all the way back to port.

The next stop was Gimli, a few miles up the western shore. Gimli is a working port settled by Icelanders about a century ago. A Viking festival and general funday was in progress when I arrived; yachts and fishing boats blended comfortably in the background. It was hard to believe that in 5 or 6 months, strong winds as cold as 60 below zero would moan across the prairie, shrouding all this in snow and ice.

About 100 miles southeast of the city of Winnipeg and perched on the Minnesota border is Lake of the Woods—a spectacular maze of islands, creeks, and backwaters. The lower 35 miles of the lake are more open; the upper half is a lacework of islands. Although the town of Kenora, Ontario, on the upper lake is busy and bustling, a sailor could easily get lost for a happy summer in the remote reaches. The winds seemed much lighter, possibly muffled by the trees. The southern shores of all these lakes are marshy and buggy at night. Good screens are in order throughout the region; the Lake of the Woods especially is a mosquito's paradise as well as a yachtsman's.

The prairie lakes are a worthy objective for Midwestern trailer sailors. I'd prefer Lake Winnipeg for real sailing, Lake of the Woods for gunkholing. Having heard virtually nothing of the area before seeing it, I'd recommend it now.

The highway to Thunder Bay, Ontario, on the northwest shore of Lake Superior was the worst I encountered. I wouldn't have wanted to tow much more than a thousand pounds through it. One section encountered in the dark was so rough that I slammed around violently, tearing one fender from the trailer.

Thunder Bay itself is a crisp, well-kept city, as are Canadian cities in

In Lake Winnipeg the children of Gimli participate in a Viking festival. Most of the townspeople here emigrated from Iceland.

general. The yacht facility is a model of friendly efficiency. Twin launch ramps and ample parking make this an ideal point of departure.

Superior is best thought of as a freshwater ocean. With 45 degree water, the lake should be treated with utmost respect. A capsize can be fatal if help isn't on the scene within 10 to 15 minutes.

The winds on Superior were light when *Fearless* and I set out. We sailed easily out halfway to Sawyer Harbor, located on the Sleeping Giant—the huge peninsula that protects Thunder Bay harbor from the violence of Superior's worst moods. Black Bay to the north offers a sandy bottom for anchoring, but it's exposed to southeast winds. Try sailing out Thunder Bay, around the Giant to Tee Harbour on the peninsula's outer shoreline, then up to the channel islands. Backwater areas warm to an almost bearable 60 degrees. You can gunkhole happily there for weeks; the bold shoreline is spectacular. Just be careful. Iron deposits throw off your compass from time to time, as do wrecked ships. The 729-foot ore carrier *Edmund Fitzgerald* is a major source of local magnetic disturbance where it lies in 530 feet of water off Whitefish Point in the southeast corner of the lake. The *Fitzgerald,* loaded with 26,000 long tons of taconite pellets, broke apart in a November, 1975 gale while trying to reach the safety of Whitefish Bay. Its 29-member crew may never be recovered. Bodies don't rise in Superior. They sink and are preserved forever in the cold. Thinking of them, I took care, while enjoying myself, not to become preserved in a similar manner.

My trip home took me along Lake Huron's north shore. The North Channel is one of North America's finest cruising grounds. Tired and anxious for home, I took notes but stayed on the highway. Heading south through Manitoulin Island, I couldn't help falling in love with the place. *Fearless* hit the water and we passed the night tied to a tree.

The next day, I pulled out and boarded a ferry for Tobermory, on the

Sailing into Lake Superior out of Thunder Bay, Ontario. The shadowy outline of "The Sleeping Giant" extends along the horizon to port; a grain ship plows into the harbor off the starboard bow.

point of the Bruce Peninsula. The area reminded me of Maine, its rugged shorelines tufted with pines. A lighthouse marked the entrance to Tobermory. Here's all the charm of Maine without the currents and the tides—and, alas, without the lobsters. The water is clear to 30 feet, fresh and clean enough to dip your cup down and drink. This purity accounts for one of the local points of interest: an underwater marine park. You can motor out of Tobermory harbor around a bend, into a cove, and dive on wrecks only 12 to 20 feet down. This was irresistible even for a jaded, homesick sailor. Besides, I had a new Canon Aquasnappy and now was the time to put it through its paces. So wetsuit be damned; over I went and dove to my first wreck. A dive boat was nearby to loan a mask and keep an eye on me.

The 45 degree water was far more bearable than I had imagined, and I investigated the wreck and the underside of my own boat for around ten minutes. Getting topside again was difficult and, once out, I toppled drunkenly to the deck. "What's happening to me?" I asked. "Hypothermia," answered a diver. "We had our eye on you. A few more minutes and you wouldn't have made it up the ladder." Step two, I learned, was a crashing, debilitating headache. "Then what?" I asked. "Then you die." the diver replied. Here's a thought for cold-water sailors: Visit a dive shop and get a rubber hood for your head, it will reduce drastic heat loss from your most vulnerable area. While you're there, get rubber booties and rubber gloves. These fit into the smallest of boats. Space permitting, a vest would be the next item of choice, but even hood, booties, and gloves can at least double or triple your survival time in cold water, and maybe save your life.

Tied to a tree off Manitoulin Island, Lake Huron.

I not only learned something in Tobermory, I fell in love with the place too. It's not so far away I can't go back and have my family along when I do.

When *Fearless* was out of the water, I had a mug of coffee, buckled up and considered my trip over. I reentered the U.S. at Niagara Falls, which hardly earned a sideways glance, and hot-footed across Route 90 for Boston. The Finger Lakes region is a lovely area, but New Yorkers will have to forgive me if, after all I had seen, I didn't linger. Violent thunderstorms helped keep me awake, and then familiar things along the road buoyed me for the final stretch. I turned the stereo up loud, tapped my feet in time, and let my mind wander in gratitude for my wife and children and all the things we had seen in 48 days. I had piles of notes and more than 30 rolls of film to process. The next day, I checked my odometer, and after driving around the block three times had a neat 10,000 miles on it. Home again.

I have come to believe the key to traveling is not in taking in the countryside like we take in a movie—as a higher form of entertainment or even self-improvement. It lies instead in releasing yourself fully to inhabit the space you're in to the best of your ability—in opening your heart to loving everything you see, so the more you see, the more you are expanded.

A travel brochure for Lake Powell promises "an eternity in an afternoon," a well-meaning but dishonest promise. Even God could not do that. Being only human, we do well when we can experience a full afternoon in an afternoon. Travel helps us learn how to do that, too.

Very early in our trip, we stopped for the night in a campground in Virginia. As I returned to *Fearless* from the laundry, a little window on a camper snapped open and an elderly woman's face appeared, fringed with steel-colored hair frizzy as a Brillo pad. "Where are you going?" I laid out for her the whole itinerary as it stretched before us. "That's *super,*" she said. "You'll love it. The good Lord has arranged this country so the very best places cannot be reached by motor car."

And that, my friend, is the central point of my story.

CHAPTER 2

Planning Your Trip

PERHAPS YOU LIVE in Arizona and dream of waking in a cool lake high in the Rocky Mountains, or maybe you live in Minnesota and imagine sailing in Mexico's Gulf of California. Or you're in West Virginia and want to pull your boat onto the sands of a Cape Cod beach. Can't you just pack your stuff and go? Does every adventure have to be planned like the Invasion of Normandy? Whatever happened to good old serendipity, the art of letting things unfold as they will?

The Serendipity Approach

Try this first on nearby places. If you can't keep a few changes of clothes and a small pile of canned goods aboard your boat at all times, have a "sailing duffel" in the house for each member of the family and a "galley box" of edibles, plastic plates and utensils, a pot and pan, and a camping stove. Now you can be off in a flash whenever the spirit moves you.

Then try this some weekend: Get out a road atlas and make a list of lakes and other interesting sailing places. Write these on scraps of paper, mix them in a hat, and select one. This way, there are no arguments. The process has a quick and light touch to it. If the family seems to like it, you can even commit to much longer trips in the same way, especially if the process of getting all the necessary items together becomes almost automatic. If you're going to do this, and the kids have an imaginative and humorous streak, let them guess, as the miles roll by, where you're actually going. Toss them a road atlas and let them tick off the landmarks you pass until educated guesses start floating forward from the back seat. This is a nice way to teach a little informal geography. Kids enjoy thinking their parents are a little crazy, as long as they don't think you're dangerous.

Planning Ahead

Long-distance trips benefit from planning. If you have all winter to plan for the summer's trip, why not use the time to gather information? You'll be amazed at the enormous amount of informative stuff you can get for free. Being able to visualize your destination in advance gives you opportunities to savor your trip over and over before you've even begun it.

Advance routing will help you anticipate how much time your trip will take. You may be tempted to sample the maximum number of places, devoting a day or two to each, but I recommend you not leave a place until everybody is restless to move on. There's no way you can see *everything* anyway; don't flog yourself and your family trying.

Planning creates opportunities for domestic democracy. Everybody can study the incoming information and offer suggestions. If your kids are more passive and indifferent than you'd like, don't worry about it. Give them a place in the discussion, but when you see them roll their eyes heavenward, allow them to be excused. It's a temptation to expect them to approach our contributions to their educations with breathless eagerness, and to experience scenic vistas with rapture. Try to resist anticipating how your kids will react. They'll see what they see and get what they get. If they knew in advance what to expect and how to feel about it, they wouldn't be kids. Now, our daughters remember (and miss) some of the beautiful places we visited. At the time, though, the single and always dependable attraction to any location was a good waterslide. They became connoisseurs. Travel brochures love to show kids on local waterslides. Be sure to point these out.

Serendipity Versus Planning: Summary

There are virtues to planning, and to trusting your destiny to the open road. May I suggest both. Plan ahead as meticulously as you can, then, once you're on the highway, be prepared to chuck the most elaborate itinerary and do what you feel. After all, the only final constraints are time and money—and maybe even these are open to discussion, if you're lucky. Save *both* time and money to indulge the tastes of your children. Doing so will sweeten the trip and keep them open to appreciate the things that *you* came on the trip for.

What Will It All Cost?

The answer to this obviously depends on several variables:

• Will you be cooking a lot of your own meals? Try to be realistic about this. It's tiring enough traveling long distances, let alone cooking at the day's end. Try taking a weekend trip and cooking all your meals. If it's no special problem, you're in a good position to save money. If you find cooking a hassle—as I do—you can rationalize thus: If the air-conditioned pleasure of a restaurant meal fortifies you sufficiently that you can camp out happily for the night, then you'll save important money. Our trip took us through a lot of country so hot that a meal was an excuse to cool off for a while under an air conditioner. We cooked less than we planned until we entered the Canadian Rockies, where suddenly a fire was a source of comfort. If you're going into the wilderness or out to sea, then obviously you're going to *have* to prepare your own grub.

• How many nights will you spend in motels? We averaged one night of every four, which gave everybody a chance to bathe at leisure and enjoy more space than the van allowed. Campgrounds offer many amenities at one-fifth to one-third the price of an inexpensive motel. You miss the serenity of truly being away from it all, but it can be an economical compromise. Kids can wander, dive in a pool, find temporary companions. The *really* cheap way to overnight is to pull into a rest stop, shopping mall parking lot, road-stop parking lot—or to be in country so remote that you can pull over anywhere. The best nights are spent under the stars in your boat. And those are free.

• What kind of gas mileage does your car get? Our Toyota van averaged more than 20 miles to the gallon towing our boat. Our total gas bill for 10,000 miles was under $500. If you're trying to figure your mileage while traveling in Canada, here's a tip: To convert kilometers to miles, just look at your odometer. It's a ready-made conversion chart. Actually, 100 kilometers per hour (about 62 miles per hour) is a nice cruising speed, making arrival estimates easy. Again, take a weekend trip and calculate your mileage. Then you can budget gas realistically.

• Figure in gas, food, and lodging of all sorts, then add another 50 percent. We found money going out for books, pools, waterslides, ferry passages, extra gadgets, and God knows what all. We spent as much on the miscellaneous category as we did on food—an average of $18 a day.

Here's how our trip expenses broke down. We were out 48 days and covered 10,000 miles. Most of the time, we were three (my two daughters and me). For two weeks, we were four (when my wife could join us). For the last week, crossing the plains of Canada, I was on my own.

hotels:	$484 total	$10.00/day average
gas:	$492 total	$10.25/day average
meals:	$878 total	$18.29/day average
groceries:	$ 84 total	$1.75/day average (A huge load of food was given to us by a trucker in Alberta.)
miscellaneous:	$874 total	$18.20/day average
TOTAL	$2812	$58.49/day average

We could have done it more economically, but our car wasn't air conditioned and so we cooked less and used motels more than planned. Still, who do you know who can vacation a family on $58 a day? We did it and so can you.

See the Appendices for a sample trip ledger.

Getting Information

Typically a state or provincial tourist office will send you a colorful magazine with an overview of touring its area, often with stunning photography and a discussion of what awaits you. The magazine often will be supplemented by a bundle of brochures listing the calendar of interesting events across the state or province, and describing in more detail the state, provincial, or national parks you might visit. You get quite a lot and the information usually is detailed enough to be useful.

At the end of each chapter in Part II you'll find addresses and phone numbers for the tourist offices of the areas just covered. Here's a tip: While writing for information is fine and will produce the same result, you can cut through a great deal of bureaucracy simply by picking up the phone. In most instances the process is designed to accommodate callers, not writers, and the people on the other end of the line seem delighted to get your address and drop something in the mail. Pennsylvania and California, in fact, were unable to grasp the concept that someone may want to write for information and couldn't furnish an address. I'm not sure of the greater social significance of such a trend; perhaps no one writes anymore.

It might be helpful to mention that you are interested in sailing; you may get a brochure on specifics along with the general stuff.

ADDITIONAL INFORMATION

AAA. You can complement the information from government agencies in any number of ways. It's well worth your while to join the American (or Canadian) Automobile Association, even if you're not planning a major trip. You get free towing and rescue service, even cash advances with certain memberships. See them while you're still in the early planning stages of a trip; they can provide very specific and useful information. They'll map out a "Triptik," a master plan that will recommend scenic or speedy highways, break down the trip into reasonable driving days, list campgrounds along your route, and give you tons of highway maps.

Campground Directories. Visit your local bookstore (sometimes a well-equipped sporting goods store) and browse among the travel atlases. There are a number of directories that list campgrounds and detail what services and facilities each provides and what each costs. Pick whatever looks good; you have a wide choice.

Other Books and Services. You'll find a list of specific books, and where to get them, in the Appendices.

CHAPTER 3

Choosing a Boat

IF YOU DON'T already own a boat, figuring out what to buy may seem like a horribly complicated business. If you ask for advice, you'll get lots—all of it passionate, and all of it different. Expect people to disagree strenuously about size, make, rig, hull type. Consult also your subconscious. Sailing is an essentially romantic pastime; God knows, it isn't practical. So when you dream of sailing somewhere, what kind of boat are you on? The boat you see when you close your eyes is the one you really want. Can't afford the boat you see? Then try to find yourself a little one that somehow reminds you of it. If you get a boat that doesn't spark your emotions, you'll find an excuse to sell it in an impractically short time. Honest.

Having said that, there remain a number of practical considerations. Let's introduce several basic types of boats and then ask several useful questions.

Cartoppable Boats

There are a number of lightweight boats and sailing canoes that can be carried on the roof of your car. You need no trailer, no boat ramp. Some of these boats are fast sailers. You'll have to be happy about getting wet sometimes. Sleeping on the floor of a canoe isn't my idea of a good time; best sleep in tents ashore. In wilderness areas, you can do that, but you can't pitch a tent in the parking lot of a Howard Johnson's along Interstate 90. This is a good idea for rugged outdoor types or for getting into really remote or inaccessible areas. For rough water areas, you'll need completely waterproof pouches for your sleeping bags and other gear. It's the simplest way to go—and the least expensive.

Small Open Boats

There is quite a variety of small open boats available. You may need a light trailer, but well-secured gear can be carried permanently in the boat, reducing congestion in the car. If you're a traditionalist, there are several dories and other designs available that not only will sail well but add a touch of romance. These will be easy to manhandle. With no cabin, you'll have to improvise some sort of cockpit shelter or plan to sleep ashore.

Micro-cruisers

You can buy very small boats with cuddy cabins that sleep two. Deck and cockpit space will be smaller than on an open boat of the same length, but the cabin is always there. You can sleep in the boat underway or use it as a camper while on the road. This kind of boat is my most frequently chosen vessel for the traveling we've done. Micro-cruisers make effortless trailering, and with some kind of cockpit tent, you can even bring your kids overnight, too.

Compact Cruisers

Compact cruisers usually will have double the sleeping capacity of the micro-cruisers and about twice the weight. (They'll weigh about 1,000 pounds.) You'll get more elbow room, more storage, and more amenities. Trailering is still relatively easy, although you'll certainly be more aware

A catamaran with a storage module mounted forward of the trampoline.

Left: Bettina sails Fearless, *our Potter 15, in the Canadian Rockies. Right: the Com-pac 16 barrels along with a sailor and his dog.*

of the load. If you're planning to spend extended time aboard, the extra room makes a big difference.

Multihulls

These boats are light and easy to trailer and manhandle. If you like high performance and aren't going to be sailing where floating logs or underwater obstructions might bring you to a crashing halt, these fast boats are an attractive option. Store camping gear in a light plastic box or in waterproof bags. I've heard of a custom camping tent called a "Hobie Hilton," but I've never seen one. You could rig your own shelter and sleep on the trampoline.

There are bigger boats that can be trailered, but if you're really going to drag your boat all around the country—especially if you're going up to mountain lakes and down poorly paved road surfaces, a heavy boat will be a ball and chain. Think small and light. Go anywhere. (The fragility of the small-boat manufacturing business makes it difficult to guarantee that all these boats are still in production. Look for *features* that other manufacturers may have incorporated. Check out the used boat market. There are some good bargains out there.)

Some Good Boats (Trailerable and Under $9,000)
MICRO-CRUISERS
The West Wight Potter 15. The little Potter is actually 14 feet long. It weighs in at 450 pounds, making it by far the lightest and most easily hauled boat in its class. It's faster than it looks, and is remarkably stable and free of spray. Potter 15s have been sailed transatlantic and from the West Coast to Hawaii. Their cabins are snug, but have two honest berths. They are character boats, and not everybody will like them, but those who do often have loyalty bordering on the fanatic.
Length: 14 feet; beam: 5¹/₂ feet; weight: 450 pounds; draft: 7 inches (centerboard up)/3¹/₂ feet (centerboard down).
H.M.S. Marine, 904 W. Hyde Park Blvd., Inglewood, CA 90302

The Com-pac 16. This seems to be the other national bestseller. The Com-pac has a shoal keel. Virtues: simplicity, more ultimate stability, and

no centerboard trunk in the cabin. Very solid construction. Differences: It's almost three times the Potter's weight to haul around, and it requires a deeper launch ramp to float the boat off the trailer. The cabin has superior layout for a portable toilet, but the bunks are more cramped. It's a stiff and secure sailer with more than 7 feet of cockpit space.
Length: 16 feet; beam: 6 feet; weight: 1,100 pounds; draft 1½ feet. Hutchins Co. Inc., 1195 Kapp Drive, Clearwater, FL 33515

The Peep Hen. Here's an odd-looking boat with logic all its own. Designed by small boat wizard Reuben Trane on a New Year's Eve, the Peep has astonishing room below and a "summer cabin" (tent system) that neatly and completely encloses the cockpit. The simple unstayed rig goes up in a trice. The Peep has a flat bottom, giving it a very stable ride. It's not designed for particularly rough or hostile conditions. You can get it with a heavy Plexiglass window *in the bottom!*
Length: 14 feet; beam: 6½ feet; weight: 1,000 pounds; draft: 15 inches (centerboard up)/3 feet (centerboard down). Mirage Fiberglass, P.O. Drawer 1489, Palatka, FL 32078-1489

The Nordica 16. The Nordica has been around for more than a decade. Its hull form is definitely Old World. She'd be a good sea boat. Actually, the Nordica has a keel no deeper than that of the Com-pac 16, so the boat is more at home in shoal water than it looks. The cockpit is unusually deep and protected, but it's not self-bailing. Water that gets in, even rainwater, must be pumped out. Opinions about self-bailing are mixed; many prefer the comfort of the deep well. If I had a Nordica, I'd try to

The Peep Hen 14.

figure out how to self-bail the boat. At 925 pounds the Nordica 16 isn't too much to haul around. It's definitely pretty!

Length: 16 feet; beam: 6 feet 2 inches; weight: 925 pounds; draft: 1 foot 8 inches.

Nordica Yachts, Highway 14, Mount Brydges, Box 339, Ontario, CANADA N0L 1W0

The Montgomery 15. The Montgomery may well be the swiftest of the micro-cruisers. The tall rig and fine entry do well. Fiberglass lapstrakes are more than cosmetic; they stiffen the hull. At least one Montgomery has joined the Potters in trekking from California to Hawaii. The cabin has two berths in a vee with storage under the cockpit seats. The Montgomery features a keel drawing 15 inches, with a centerboard housed inside the keel for windward work.

Length: 15 feet; beam: 6½ feet; weight: 750 pounds; draft: 15 inches (centerboard up)/3 feet (centerboard down).

Montgomery Marine, 3236 Fitzgerald Road, Unit 1, Rancho Cordova, CA 95670

Left: the Nordica 16 bashes along in a stiff breeze. Right: the Montgomery 15 under sail.

COMPACT CRUISERS

The Seaward 18 "Fox". Here's a boat with the huge cockpit of the traditional catboats but with a modern hull form under the waterline. She's a good sailing boat, stiff and more speedy than her beam would suggest. A fully battened sail and shoal-draft wing keel combine some new thinking with traditional simplicity. Although the boat sleeps four, I'd adapt the cabin to create luxury for two and sleep the kids under a boom-tent.

Length on deck: 17 feet; beam: 8 feet; weight: 1,200 pounds; draft: 19 inches.
Starboard Yacht Co., 4550 S.E. Hampton Court, Stuart, FL 34997.

The West Wight Potter 19. I think this boat has more livable room below for the weight than any production boat around in 1989. With its optional "short rig" that carries the sail area in a lower profile, the mast can be raised with one hand. The hard-chined, high-sided hull makes for a stiff, dry ride. In high winds, reef early to ease the helm. Drawbacks: The cockpit is snug at 5½ feet; only children could sleep out there. And I'm convinced that the 370-pound steel daggerboard could be safely replaced with a fiberglass board, and a winch system replaced with a simple lanyard.

Length: 18½ feet; beam: 7½ feet; weight: 1,200 pounds; draft: 6 inches (retractable keel up)/3½ feet (retractable keel down).
(See Potter 15 for manufacturer's address.)

The Saroca. It's ironic that one of the most versatile small craft built anywhere should be considered a "specialty" item. The Saroca is designed

The Potter 19 cruising in California.

for rowing, paddling, and sailing. You can cartop it, camp along the shoreline with it, even set up a snug custom cover and sleep on its sole. For someone interested in really roughing it, with one of these and a four-wheel-drive vehicle, there is hardly any water you couldn't get to. For information, write to:

Saroca, 27 Hedly Street, Portsmouth, RI 02871; phone 401-683-9003.

The Sovereign 17. A number of good small sailboats have gone out of production. Here's a deserving survivor. The Sovereign 17 can look a little boxy from certain angles, but the shape provides for a commodious interior, cleverly set up for cruising. A couple could like this. The boat looks best with a dark green hull and buff decks. An ingenious boom gallows also assists in raising and lowering the mast. This shoal-keel boat weighs about 1,200 pounds.

Custom Fiberglass Products of Florida, Inc., 8136 Leo Kidd Ave., Port Richey, FL 34668; phone 813-847-5798.

SMALL OPEN BOATS

The Dovekie. Here's an ultralight, highly innovative 21-footer. It has leeboards and draws only 4 inches with them up!

Write Edey & Duff, 129 Aucoot Road, Mattapoisett, MA 02739.

Left: the Sovereign 17.
Right: small open boats...
the Dovkie.

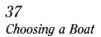

Drascombe of England produces several small, but seaworthy, open boats—the smallest being the lug-rigged Scaffie.

The Melonseed. This is a very traditional 14-footer, pretty and fast. The Melonseed uses a sprit rig—a wonderful small-boat sailplan. The same builder makes a fiberglass version of the traditional dory.
Write Crawford Boat Building, Box 430, Humarock, MA 02047.

There are other good boats out there. I've limited my discussion here to boats that weigh 1,200 pounds or less—that are really portable behind average cars. *Small Boat Journal* and *Sail*'s annual sailboat and equipment directories are good sources of information about products. Or you can write: **Yankee Boat Works,** Box 670, 21 Rockland Place, Stamford, CT

This may be one of the most capable and affordable cartop boats available. Howmar's Delta weighs 185 pounds—a handful but still light enough to hoist onto a wagon or a van. Courtesy Howmar Boats, Edison, NJ.

06904; **American Sail,** 7350 Pepperdam Avenue, Pepperdam Industrial Park, Charleston, SC 29418 (a good catamaran too!); **Howmar Boats,** Box 7112, Edison, NJ 08818 (Ask about the new Delta.); and, **Old Town Canoes, Grumman Aluminum Canoes.** (See local dealers for the best deals. Other brands may be made close to you.)

My list covers boats and/or boat builders I have had personal contact with. I do not wish to imply that boats not listed are necessarily inferior in some way.

Equipping Your Boat for Long-Distance Cruising

While most small boats come from the factory ready to sail away, they're certainly not ready to cruise in. What else do you need?

THE RIG

Many small boats have no provision for holding up the boom when the sails are lowered. The whole mess falls into the cockpit. You can easily rig a *topping lift* to hold up the boom. Basically, it's a line running from the masthead to the end of the boom, set so that it's a little slack when the sail is raised. If you run lines on *both* sides of the sail to the boom, you've got *lazyjacks* that will keep the sail from falling all over the place when lowered.

It's a good idea to get a pop-riveting tool for jobs like this. Things go quickly and easily.

If you get longer halyards, and a couple of pulleys and cleats, you can lead your halyards from the base of the mast back to the after edge of the cabin roof. Now you can raise sail without ever leaving the cockpit.

Most sails come from the factory with a boltrope sewn to the edge of the sail. This fits into a groove in the mast when the sail is raised. When the sail comes down, it falls all over the place. You can't raise it in a

Lazyjacks hang slightly slack when the sail is raised. When the sail is lowered, the lazyjacks hold up the boom and keep the sail from falling all over the cockpit and cabintop.

Some useful hardware—a sail slug and sail stop.

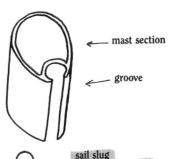

←— mast section

←— groove

sail slug
(These are sewn every 2 feet along the sail. The slugs instead of the boltrope fit into the mast groove.)

sail stop
(After all the slugs are fed into the mast groove, the stop is fitted into place and screwed down tight to keep the slugs from falling out when the sail is lowered.)

hurry—especially in high winds. I have always put *slugs* at intervals along the edge of the sail. These fit into the mast slot, and a *sailstop* is screwed in just above the opening in the slot to keep the slugs from falling out when the sail is lowered. Now you can lower sail and it won't fall out, and you can get underway again promptly. This is seamanlike.

THE COCKPIT

It's good to put down a *cockpit grating* so sand and grit aren't ground into the fiberglass floor. Shoes tend to stay drier too.

You can purchase teak *grab rails* through marine catalog houses. Adding one to the top of the hatch slide provides a firm grip. I've added pairs flanking the companionway hatch and another pair flanking the forward hatch for added security. (Children especially need this.)

A permanently mounted *fold-down swim ladder* should be standard on every boat. If your boat didn't come with one, add one.

SAFETY EQUIPMENT

You'll need an anchor, line, a compass, lights for night sailing, a good flashlight, a horn, life jackets, flares, and charts for the areas you'll be sailing.

Fold-down boarding ladders should be standard equipment on all sailboats.

THE CABIN

To store your gear, you'll need to use the walls of your cabin effectively. Monkey hammocks can be fastened to the liner with pegboard hooks or eye fittings pop-riveted in, as can *satchels* and other small bags. Now the beds are clear.

A *paper towel rack* is really handy. Velcro is handy stuff with which to attach all kinds of things to the cabin walls, including a compass, *battery-powered closet lights,* and *mosquito netting* covering all the openings to the cabin such as air scoops and ventilators.

If your vee berth has a center cutaway, consider a *filler-cushion* to bridge the gap and provide better shoulder room. An "orgy-board" one sailor called it. Do you have quarter berths? Consider mounting Beckson's *inspection ports* on either side of the cockpit footwell to ventilate them. Footwells can get close and hot.

Consider *cockpit tents, dodgers, biminis,* and all other forms of shelter that might turn your cockpit into a protected area—a living room.

Is your ventilation going to be adequate? Nicro-Fico makes all sorts of *ventilators, air scoops,* and even *solar-powered ventilators.* Especially when it rains and you have to close your hatches, effective vents can make all the difference.

Do you have an effective way to call for help? A *marine radio* might offer some security. If you're thinking of a long coastal or ocean sail, an *Emergency Position-Indicating Radio Beacon* (EPIRB) is vital. When activated it transmits an emergency signal on preset frequencies to aircraft and satellites, or to VHF radio receivers; your position can be fixed easily and accurately.

Outfitting your boat for extensive cruising may cost you around 20 percent the value of your boat, but then you'll have a compact home on the water, and the amenities of a bigger and *much* more expensive boat.

Waking up in a sunny Florida inlet, a far cry from the snows of this youngster's native Michigan.

CHAPTER 4

The Gypsy Caravan

YOU'LL KNOW YOU'VE perfected your rig (your boat and automobile) when your house could burn down and you could accomplish life's functions on a very modest scale without it. This means that everybody would have a dry place to lie down, a place to store personal stuff, a place to store food and cook it, places to sit, and a place to go to the bathroom and clean up . . . all in a small boat and a van or car! How do you do that?

Some of this you'll accomplish with cleverness; some of this you'll accomplish by reducing your expectations about the material requirements for happiness. It is not enough for you to make the adjustments; your *family* also must be interested in adjusting, or living like gypsies won't work. After all, your kids were not born gypsies, nor have you probably raised them as such.

Privacy is going to be the most precious commodity. Sleeping two in a van and two in a boat can provide at least a generational separation during your nights on the road. When you're in campgrounds or camping on beaches you might want to bring tents for the kids. Ask the kids before you put a lot of money into equipment. On the whole, you'll feel abnormally cramped. Maybe you can go to a theater and everybody can see a different movie. If your kids are old enough, you can find a mall where they can wander around on their own. Please don't cringe at that suggestion. Teenagers are connoisseurs of malls and are apt to have less of an urge to "get away from it all" than you do. In safe, natural settings, there are more serene chances to be alone too.

Don't overlook the Walkman as a form of auditory privacy. Keep lots of batteries on hand. We stopped at bookstores every day or so for the girls to refresh their supply of reading materials. We planned for a bottomless book budget. The girls swapped books, exchanged opinions on the plots and characters, and occasionally asked me to read a book so they could get another opinion. This is good stuff to have going on in your family.

If you have a boat with four bunks, your automobile may just be a place to sit down. Personally, I feel a van with beds is an invaluable addition to the caravan concept and I'd only do a trip without one if I were going alone. With a micro-cruiser, you can't sleep a family of four unless you either sleep two people ashore in tents or adapt the cockpit for sleeping. Lay two oak or teak strips along the upper edges of the cockpit footwell. Through-bolt them in place. Then cut a couple of plywood sections to fit. (You can store them flat under bunk cushions when they're not in use.) Now, you can cover the cockpit and inflate air matresses.

Shelter

A cockpit tent is a necessity on any small boat. Making full use of your cockpit is vastly less expensive than buying a bigger boat. You can do a fair job with cheap rip-stop nylon tarp, improvising tie-down points to hold it in place. With a simple frame, you can open up more space. Arc some 1/2-inch flexible plumber's pipe over the cockpit and slip its ends over V-clamps mounted on each coaming. Several hoops across the cockpit resemble an old Conestoga wagon—and serve the same purpose. A tarp can be stretched across the framework, turning the whole area

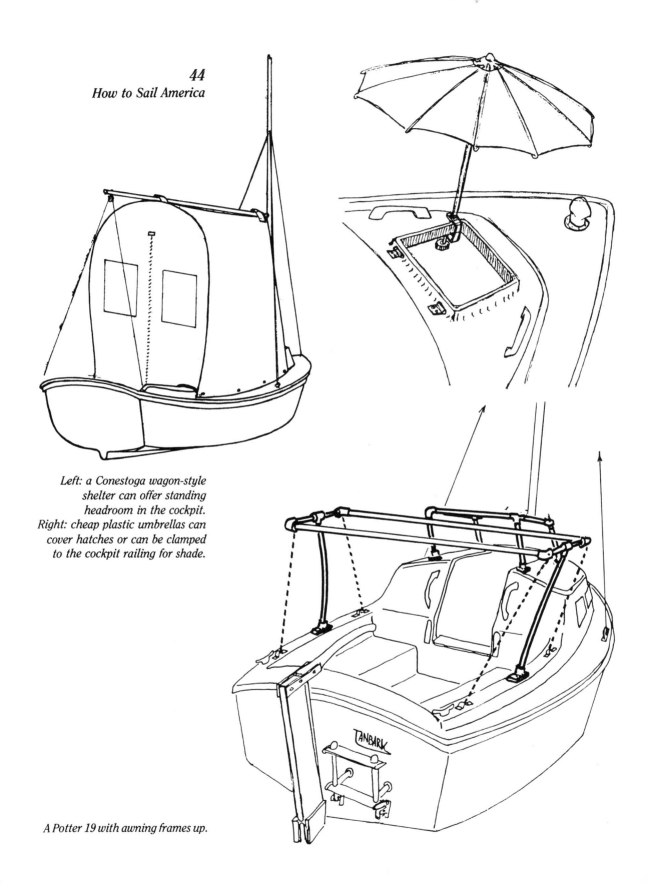

Left: a Conestoga wagon-style shelter can offer standing headroom in the cockpit. Right: cheap plastic umbrellas can cover hatches or can be clamped to the cockpit railing for shade.

A Potter 19 with awning frames up.

beneath into a living room for a sailing couple or a second bedroom for kids.

Cooking Under Way

Your kitchen is best stored in a box under one of the cockpit seats. We've used a $12 propane camping stove. With nestling pots, we can cook rice in the bottom one and warm soup in a second one perched atop the first. (Someone needs to steady this.) Propane stoves cook with a hotter flame than do alcohol stoves; you can make pancakes on a propane stove. Pressurized alcohol stoves have been known to cause cabin fires that burn with an invisible flame and therefore go undetected for a serious length of time. *Un*pressurized alcohol stoves seem safer to me. If your cooking needs will be few and simple, Sterno stoves collapse almost into nothing and are essentially foolproof. In any case, you should have a small fire extinguisher aboard at all times. If your cabin has no forward hatch, be prudent about cooking with the stove in the main hatchway: A cooking fire might block your family's exit from the cabin. It's best to cook with the stove somewhere in mid-cockpit—*but well away from any gasoline cans.*

On relatively short cruises, you can serve onto paper plates and bowls—using one Ziploc bag for clean plates, one for used. Uneaten food can feed the fowl and fishes, and no one has to clean. Teflon pans can be wiped clean with a paper towel. Make space for a trash bag. On *Tanbark,* our Potter 19, we don't use bowls at all; we use mugs for cereal as well as coffee, thus saving space.

Storing Gear

We always bring too much stuff along with us. Bring half as many clothes and twice as much money and you'll be fine. In good weather, we're wearing as little as social convention allows anyway. Even when I sailed *Tanbark* for a month, I found clothes I had never worn when I unpacked.

The key to storing your gear in a small boat is to use the walls of the cabin. Monkey hammocks keep gear where you can see it—and mildew free. You also can hang knapsacks from the inside of the hull. That way, the beds are kept clear at all times for sleeping. Anchors and line can be hung from the bow pulpit. A flashlight can be clipped to the overhead with broom clips; battery-powered closet lights can be given several useful locations with Velcro strips.

When Nature Calls

I know that many good marine writers boast that they "bucket and chuck-it," but I hope you won't do that. Portable toilets, if cleaned regularly, permit you to go to the bathroom in port or even by the side of the road. The bottom half can be discreetly emptied down a gas station toilet when it gets full. Keep a good supply of chemicals on board. Keep the toilet paper in a dry place, too. Finding a soggy, congealed mass of paper in the middle of the night is no fun.

We keep a portable toilet in the van as well as in the boat, since sometimes we have people sleeping in both locations while on the road.

A small propane stove—clean, safe, and surprisingly versatile.

A wooden ring lets towels hang away from the cabin wall and dry on both sides.

The head enclosure on Tanbark, *our Potter 19, also makes a simple chart table.*

Nobody I know is crazy about portable heads, but the alternative is environmentally unacceptable. We simply cannot permit others to defecate into the waters we bathe in and drink from. If sailors are to be effective advocates for the nation's waterways, we cannot be hypocrites about this.

Summary

Keep it as simple as you can. Take short trips first so that you can refine your skills and personalize your approach—and give your children a chance to develop a taste for it. Start with places where the sailing is easy, providing ample time to swim, explore, and just fool around. Try to provide pleasures for everyone and at least some privacy for everyone in the family. I know it gets more comfortable in a larger boat, but then you come to dread setting the thing up. You travel less and pay more. That's not the idea. Almost every sailor I've ever met says his boat is just a little smaller than he'd like it to be, at which point, his wife usually chimes in that the present one suits her just fine. Often, as the family boat keeps getting larger and larger, the rest of the family recedes into the background until it's "Dad's boat." When no one in the family feels intimidated by the boat, sailing remains a collective enterprise. Kids can even contemplate their *own* adventures as they get older. We trust them with the family car, why not the boat, if it's small and handy? What a great thing for a kid to look forward to!

Wheels: Choosing a Vehicle to Get You Down the Road

Let's assume for a moment that you're shopping for a car right now and considering some kind of sail America trip. Is there such a thing as an ideal vehicle, and if so, what would it be?

Well, it depends. How many of you are going? How big a boat are you taking; how heavy is it? Will you be sleeping in the boat, in the car, or both? How much money do you have to spend?

Ideally, I'd recommend a van with an automatic transmission; automatics adapt better to pulling a load. Boat ramps are tough on clutches. Since Toyota Motors was willing to assist us on our 10,000-mile trip, we took its minivan. It pulled our Potter 15 happily and drags our current boat, a Potter 19, with equal ease (though less gas-efficiently). For reasons of economy, we got the utility van. I built a carpeted platform onto which 7-inch-thick foam foldout chair/beds happened to fit nicely. This way, one passenger could sit up while another naps. Maximum comfort— no arguments. There was room for a portable toilet, four plastic storage bins, and four monkey hammocks hanging above the windows in back. Plastic laundry pouches hung from the back of the two forward seats. A security box under the back end of the bed permitted me to lock up valuables where no one could get at them—and leave the windows open when the car was unattended. Such an idea would be generally adaptable to most of the domestic minivans as well. Measure to make sure you've got at least six feet behind the front seats, so people can stretch out.

Make sure also that the vehicle you're looking at is designed to take a trailer hitch. My Toyota was not, and U-Haul had to adapt a fender hitch

This Volkswagen camper model uses its interior volume more effectively than any van I've seen.

to the van. (U-Haul does an efficient and reasonably priced job, by the way. If you need a towing ball put on, give them a try.) Your van can probably pull more than the specifications suggest, but you may void your guarantee if you don't conform to official suggestions.

One of the big American-made vans will pull heavier loads and will have a lot more room. Gas mileage, obviously, will not be as good. The minivans have pushed some larger vans onto the used market; there are some good deals out there. Generally, the less comfortable your boat's accommodations, the more you'll depend on your car for sleeping. With some Velcro screen kits, you can bugproof your van or car windows. In some places, this is a *must*.

Perhaps you already have a car. Unless you plan to camp out or sleep in motels every night you're on the road, you'll have to select a boat that offers you both a dry place to lie down and one to go to the bathroom, should the urge come upon you. Many cars have passenger-side front seats that recline almost fully. See if some kind of collapsible footrest can be built to support your feet while you sleep. I've seen some old cars turned into campers for one or two by ripping out the back seats completely and extending foot room into the trunk. A solo driver could remove the right front seat and run a sleeping platform from the trunk to the dashboard. If you're short on money, you can get a big gas-guzzler cheaply, then do major surgery on the insides to get what you want.

If you are taking kids on a long trip in a family sedan, schedule frequent breaks for snacks, swimming pools, waterslides, etc. In excess, life in the back seat can be hard to take.

For my family's extended trip, I wish we'd put in air conditioning. Not only was the heat punishing, but so was the continuous thunder and whine of the interstate. Sound can beat you down. At the risk of taxing your engine, consider air conditioning. It was less of a frill than I'd thought. It could transform your trip, especially if you're traveling in the South or the Southwest.

How about a camper? If you already own one, please don't let what appears to be my prejudice put you off. Campers make sense, especially if your tastes run to sailing canoes or cartoppable boats with no accommodations at all. I've seen too many of these big things with the flicker of T.V. light in the windows, air conditioned and hermetically sealed like spaceships. It is my private belief that one goes out into the wilderness with as much simplicity and with as few distractions as possible. For children especially, who have yet to see so many things, television erects a barrier between sense and environment. I urge you to leave the electronic media at home so the natural world has at least a tiny chance to make its impression. The root of the word "vacation" is "vacate"— to leave, to exit from, to empty. To go on a vacation, we not only have to vacate our usual address; we have to empty ourselves of at least some of the routine things that make up ordinary life—so there will be openings for the new and unexpected things we find en route.

Trailering and Launching Your Boat

There's a good chance that whoever sold you your boat and trailer included an owner's manual for the trailer. That's a good document to look over.

Hauling your boat down the highway is probably the most hazardous part of the whole sailing operation. Let's face it; you're traveling at least *ten times* faster than you ever will under sail. What should you be mindful of?

- Your trailer is affixed to the rear end of your car. It would be an unimaginable calamity if it should part company from your car at highway speeds. Make sure your hitch is more than adequate for the load you're pulling. Have safety chains *crossed* under the hitch, in case the ball and socket coupling ever lets go. Inspect the coupling frequently to make sure that vibration or stress hasn't damaged it in some way.
- Your car is not going to accelerate as rapidly with the boat attached—and more to the point, *it won't brake as effectively* either. When there's no traffic near you, try braking at speed to see your capabilities. Leave a lot of room between you and the cars ahead. Have your brakes checked before leaving on a long trip. On long downgrades downshift, letting the engine's compression ease you downhill rather than burning out your brakes trying to keep things under control.
- Find an empty parking lot and practice backing with your trailer. In reverse, swing the *underside* of your wheel in the same direction you want the boat to go. Avoid oversteering. Once the trailer gets at too acute an angle, it simply won't behave. While backing up, make adjustments in gradual intervals; it works better that way.
- When you get to your launch ramp, it's often easier to set the boat up while you're still on terra firma, so long as you're not blocking the

A boat on its trailer poised to back down the ramp.

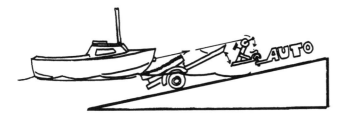

launch

A tilting device can really help you on shallow ramps. You lift the bow of the boat and dump the boat in.

When you winch the boat back on, be sure the centerboard's pulled up.

pad

tie firmly

tie firmly

Tie down the boat before driving away. Pad areas where the line will chafe.

trailer tilt-up release

You'll find it on the tongue, under the bow of the boat. Pull the pin to allow the trailer to tilt up.

pull to release

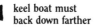

keel boat must
back down farther

Keel boats are ramp-launchable. You'll need a good ramp—or a trailer tongue extension.

way for other boaters to use the ramp. In so doing, *check for power lines overhead!* Don't raise your mast into them; don't drive your boat (and upraised mast) into them. You or one of your family can be electrocuted in so doing. Please be careful. Be sure your mast is raised securely too. Small boat masts aren't really heavy, but they weigh more than baseball bats—and they have far more leverage.

• If you have not yet ordered your boat, see if you can get the trailer tongue extended two feet longer than standard. See also if a local trailer shop can lower the bunks that support your boat, or mount the axle on top of the leaf springs—anything you can do to safely lower the boat's waterline closer to the roadbed. On poor ramps, anything helps. There are public ramps that force you to back your boat halfway into the harbor to float it off.

• When retrieving your boat, be sure again that your path out is clear of power lines. Make sure that the mast and boom are securely tied down and that your anchor (if it lives on the bow pulpit) has a safety line on it should it shake loose. Vibration is the mortal enemy of trailers. Have the necessary wrenches and walk around your boat before each day of each trip, making sure everything is tight. Especially check wheel lug-nuts for tightness. Your boat should be secured to the trailer with tie-down straps. Place pads where needed to make sure the straps don't chafe grooves into the boat's fiberglass.

• Have your wheel bearings checked at least every spring and before any major trip. Bearing Buddies are a must, as they squeeze a continuous supply of grease into bearings. That keeps corrosive water out—and keeps your wheels on. *When bearings burn out, wheels fall off!* Don't neglect them.

• Just in case your winch should let go, tie a safety line from the boat's towing eye to the trailer. This is especially important with roller-bunked trailers that permit the load to slide off easily. I've seen

There are a number of shallow-draft boats that are easy to launch, such as my Potter 19.

a motorboat neatly unload itself onto a highway at turnpike speeds. From a safe distance, it was an entertaining sight, though I'm sure the owner didn't think so.

• Consider carrying a spare tire so a flat doesn't leave you stranded. Not every gas station has replacements for little doughnut trailer tires.

• In general, let caution and vigilance become second nature when you're trailering your boat. None of this advice takes too much time. This is one area where you really don't want any problems.

If you cruise the boat shows, you'll see all sorts of boats advertised as "trailerable." I think we need three levels of trailerability whose use truth in advertising would require:

Trailerable I. The boat can be fitted with a heavy-duty trailer equipped with surge brakes. A heavy van or light truck can transport the boat successfully cross-country on major highways. With a hoist and assistance stepping the mast, the boat can be launched at most boatyards at your preferred destination. Boats up to 30 feet can be mobilized in this way.

Trailerable II. The boat can be transported behind a 6-cylinder vehicle down major highways and launched without professional assistance. Raising the mast can be accomplished either by an athletic couple or with the aid of a mast-hoisting winch system of some kind. Family weekenders in the 22-foot range fall into this category. A family can transport and launch this class of boat on its own—but not casually.

Trailerable III. This class of boat is light enough to be hauled and launched by really small cars or transported down rural roadways without difficulty. An individual can launch this class of boat alone. Daysailing for a few hours' fun on the water—transport, launch, sail, recover, return— is worth the trouble with this class boat.

For the purposes of this book, we'll be thinking of the third category mostly. You can do it with bigger boats, but it's a drag.

Traveling with Kids

Is there such a thing as a "perfect age" for young travelers? No, there are several. Infants whose health and dispositions invite you to take them places are ideal papoose companions. They won't come away with lasting memories or make funny remarks you can quote later, but from *your* point of view, it can be fairly easy. Remember that little bodies overheat faster, get cold faster, and dehydrate faster than adult bodies. This will be true of children in general. A capsize on Lake Superior (45 degrees Fahrenheit) could kill an infant, even if the child inhaled no water at all. Be very prudent.

I think the most difficult age for traveling with children is the interval after they become rapid walkers and climbers and before they reach what used to be called "the age of reason." Children between these two thresholds cannot sleep in the cockpit under a boomtent, for example, because you have no assurance that they might not crawl overboard in the middle of the night. In general, small children require someone's continuous attention. It might be a good idea to study your boat and optimize it for singlehanding, so that one person can do everything to keep the boat going while one keeps an eye out for the child.

Take a look below and see if there are any sharp corners that might need padding in case a child should fall. Can there be a space for some of the child's favorite things, maybe a quarterberth that can be not only a bed but a semiprivate cocoon?

Some kind of cockpit railing is useful to add an extra element of security. Children have smaller grips than do adults and often cannot steady themselves on the polished fiberglass surfaces that adults can grasp easily. Also, children have shorter armspans and need additional handholds to help them get around on deck. A harness for younger children can be a good idea so long as adults don't get tangled in the straps while moving across the cockpit.

Children should have on life jackets as soon as they leave the cabin, and it's not a bad idea for them to wear them while you're underway. Designate someone who can go immediately over the side in the event a child falls in. Throw a flotation cushion over the side and practice man-overboard drills, seeing how long it takes to "rescue" it. Every adult should be capable of accomplishing a rescue. Someone aboard should keep an eye on the overboard crew *at all times* so that the swimmer is not lost. The minute someone goes in, throwable cushions should be tossed out promptly.

Police whistles can be attached to jackets with a lanyard and, at night, small waterproof clip-on lamps might make the critical difference in recovering a man overboard. The cheapest life jackets are also the most bulky and uncomfortable. Let your kids select their own. Decide on a reasonable life vest policy, then stick to it. If your boat has its own flotation, *do not remove it*, looking for additional storage space. Your boat, even awash, is your best bet that you and your family can stay together, stay afloat, and be seen by help.

Small boats tend to move around a lot at anchor. It's safest if your kids swim off the stern of the boat where you can keep an eye on them and where they can't be pushed under by the hull if it swings to its anchor. The best way by far for swimmers to get back into the boat is for them to climb a fold-down ladder that's fixed permanently to the transom. Have one mounted on your boat. It's not a complicated job to do yourself. Then, even if you fall overboard accidentally, you can get back in—even if you're sailing alone.

There are other considerations to traveling with children, even older ones, that have less to do with health and safety than with issues of interest, fear, and boredom. Children have seen, on television, scenes more fantastic and mesmerizing than almost anything they'll see from the window of their family car. Even fabulous sunsets that almost reduce you to tears may seem essentially static and therefore boring to the kids. That has to be all right, at least for now. If the children sense that they have to respond to things in the same way as you do, it will cease being their trip. It will become a project and will be treated accordingly.

Car trips also jam the family together for extended periods. Find ways

Kids should get used to wearing life jackets. Get them something comfortable.

Bring along some games. Here a little table in a 17-footer is put to good use.

to permit safe *solitary* time for your kids; have one parent go off with just one child. Sometimes campgrounds offer new companions for play and chances to get some badly needed personal space. Try varying the sleeping combinations once in a while too. Bring along a book of scary stories and another book of funny stories, or make up some. Campfires crowned with starry skies are made for stories.

Try to budget money for junkfood dinners followed by a night in a motel, complete with showers and a T.V. Your kids will love you for it. If funds permit, spring for two rooms—one for you, one for them. Make a deal: dinners and T.V. in return for privacy for you and cherubic behavior from them.

There may come a time when a storm or even just rough conditions scares one of the kids. Kids have very different thresholds of fear. Laps were invented for just such occasions. Sometimes the cabin can provide much needed security. You should, in any case, establish a "battle stations" system with places for the children to go in a pinch where they won't be underfoot and you know they'll be safe. Try not to be swayed by frightened children into making unsafe decisions just to get them ashore as soon as possible. In foul weather, by all means get ashore if you can, but only when you can do so safely. Later you'll hear the story told by the frightened child about the towering waves and howling wind—*with relish*—because everything turned out all right after all.

I believe it's good also for couples to plan times when they can get away by themselves. But even then there are times when you think, "If only the kids could see this." Sometimes fights in the back seat make you think of a hand grenade going off in a 55-gallon drum. But then everything works, or one of the kids says something that just blows you away, and you remember that for the same reason we have them in the first place, we take them with us.

Leave your kids time to find solitude. Amber found a field of flowers by the shores of Lake Kinbasket.

CHAPTER 5

Attendant Considerations: Pests to Seamanship

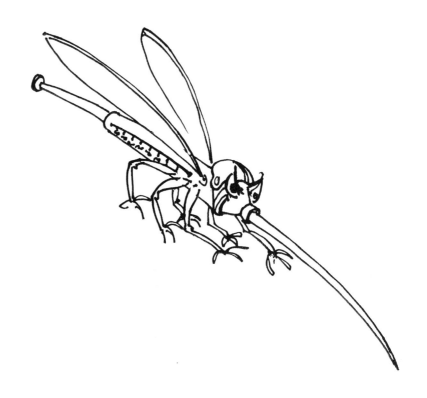

Pests

By pests, I mean anything that you don't want in your car or boat—or standing in front of you on a forest path. This category covers mosquitoes to grizzlies.

PESTS IN THE WATER

In inland waters, especially in warm, slow-moving waters, you may emerge from a swim and find leeches attached to your skin. They're loathsome little creatures, and you can't get a proper grip on them to pull them off. Your kids may freak out if they've never seen them before. Act mildly annoyed and a little bored to balance their rising panic and disgust. A little lighter fluid will get them to drop right off; keep a tin of fluid on board. A cigarette lighter flame does the trick nicely too, provided your kids can hold still for it.

Sharks. After *Jaws,* our subconscious minds will always harbor an image of us as swimmers seen from below—legs like hors d'oeuvres dangling invitingly. More Americans die of bee stings each year than of shark bite. Sharks are efficient killers but monumentally stupid. Most "attacks" are simply mistakes. Sharks have been observed actually to spit out human mouthfuls, adding insult to injury.

Most bays and shallow saltwater areas in the United States are not particularly dangerous as far as sharks are concerned. Swimming with a cut (or a menstrual period) can invite unwanted interest from sharks, as can frantic splashing on the surface, which mimics a fish in distress. In areas known to have sharks, someone should stay on deck to act as a lookout while others swim. Have a transom ladder for quick exits from the water. A frightened swimmer should stay cool and swim back to the boat *underwater* in a dignified, nonchalant way.

Kids should be reassured that while there are sharks in many waters, usually toothless sand sharks, the fear of shark attack is more a Hollywood creation than a statistical likelihood. Really.

Alligators. In southeastern waters, alligators are a reasonable cause for concern, *but only in specific places* —and not offshore. Especially in rural Florida and Georgia, ask before sailing if your route contains any locations to be wary of. Assume if you see even one that there are others and do not swim. Children and pets are more tempting targets than grown-ups.

PESTS IN THE AIR

Flies and mosquitoes won't tear off your leg (except the ones Canadians from the Northwest Territories keep telling me about), but they're a much more likely problem for you than sharks and alligators. With Velcro strips glued to the inside edges of your hatchways and sewn to the borders of flexible screens, you can protect the inside of your cabin (and car) from bugs. Citronella candles, bug coils, personal insect repellent, and spraying a bead of repellent around the edges of your screens all help keep the night mosquito-free. Don't assume that the northern latitudes are free of mosquitoes. The Arctic tundra melts on its surface in the summer, providing breeding ground for endless clouds of mosquitoes. Any area with a lot of rain provides breeding pools, so be prepared. There are medications to put on severe insect bites; check at a drugstore or camping supply house.

PESTS ON THE GROUND

Snakes. The Northeast, Midatlantic, Great Lakes, and Heartland regions of the continent are almost completely free of poisonous snakes. In the deep South, the cottonmouth, or water moccasin, is a highly poisonous and aggressively nasty creature to be avoided devoutly. It lives in swampy areas. It will go out of its way to strike passers-by—and will swim too. Ask before setting out whether there's anything to worry about. There are a few other exotic poisonous snakes that inhabit Florida in particular. The coral snake may be the worst, but it's not fast-moving, it's *very* visible with its many-colored bands, it's neither mean nor aggressive, and it lacks the fangs moccasins and rattlers have. Assuming no one is going to wait patiently while the coral snake gnaws through his epidermis, we don't have to worry about them too much, really.

In the western part of the continent, rattlers are a realistic cause for caution. Boots are a must in rattler country, as is watching the ground beneath your feet. Rattlers usually make a warning noise when disturbed, which gives you time to move carefully away. No sudden moves. Waterholes and caves sometimes have nests of rattlers. Obviously, you don't want to blunder into one. Park rangers, wilderness outfitters, sporting goods suppliers, or even the state police can let you know if there is reason for caution in the areas you plan to visit. If there is, carry a snakebite kit at all times—and read the instructions in advance, so you can react rapidly if someone is bitten.

Bears. There are some black bears in remote parts of the Eastern states and provinces, but they usually avoid human beings as best they can. Tell your kids to stay away from bear cubs, in the unlikely event they should find one. The mother bear will rush to their defense. This is true of all bears generally.

In the West and Northwest, there are grizzlies as well as black bears. These are immensely powerful animals and deserve absolute respect. Keep campsites scrupulously clean; hang food up high, out of reach. Bears are scavengers. Don't keep food in the tents you sleep in. In deep wilderness areas, you might feel more secure to anchor offshore if there are bears around. Little compressed air horns would likely scare off a curious bear; a can of Mace would be a more powerful deterrent. In grizzly country, you might consider equipping campers with a Mace can each; the same can obviously would ward off a human pest in a nonlethal way. Mace was designed for that, and it would be a less extreme burglar repellent than a flare pistol.

None of the above discussion is intended to induce paranoia. Literally millions of people travel in the wilderness every year and are bitten only by the inevitable mosquito.

How to Become an Effective Travel Photographer

Photography is a funny thing. When you go to the camera shop to pick up your pictures, you see reams and reams of newly developed photographs rolling out of the processing machines. Mostly, they seem so ordinary. If they were not your own, there would seldom be anything about them that would attract a second glance. Almost all pictures of people we care about, taken at significant times and places, have sentimental value, but how do you take pictures so good that *anyone* might value them?

Believe that what you see in the viewfinder is what you're actually going to get on the photograph. Here you are within sight of the Rocky Mountains. They run along the horizon like a distant curtain. "God, that's beautiful," you exclaim, and you grab your camera and take a picture. Weeks later, the resulting photograph reveals a 5- by 7-inch snapshot, half sky and half grass fading into the distance—and a minute band of gray squeezed in at the top. Blah. But it was so beautiful! With your *eye* you saw the mountains, and your sophisticated mind processed that view, eliminated all irrelevancies from the picture, and responded with joy and wonder to the ribbon of mountains in the distance. That is what you remember. The camera, on the other hand, had a 35-mm wide-angle lens (good for taking group photographs from a short distance) and it took in a huge panorama, of which the distant mountains were an insignificant part. Your eye is connected to your brain, your camera is not; hence the gap between your photograph and your memory. With attention and practice, your camera can become connected to your brain—a third eye—and when that happens, your photographs will become a product of your intelligence and character, just like your memories.

Practice looking at things through your camera's viewfinder. Forget what you know is out there; look only with the camera's eye. Find out how your camera sees things. If your camera has several lenses, study them all. You don't even need film, just time and patience. Walk around and check things out. Strangers won't think you're crazy; they'll think you're taking pictures.

Don't be afraid to stand your camera on end. Some people always hold their cameras flat. But some pictures are vertical. Boats are, faces are too. Church spires are vertical. Experiment.

Don't be afraid to get really close. This is especially true when photographing people. Look how close fashion magazines get to their subjects. Look for details as well as panoramas. It helps to have a tele-photo lens, so you don't literally have to breathe down your subjects' necks, but if you can't afford all that, any 50-mm lens or larger can even do attractive portraits, if you get close enough. Understand that without telephoto lenses, distant objects will play little part in the picture, no matter how attractive.

Develop a sense of foreground and background. Scenic shots often combine a prominent foreground of something interesting backed up by a scenic panorama. Try getting under a tree and framing a distant view with a fringe of close-up foliage, or crouch and put a couple of flowers in

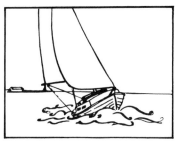

Most people are used to holding cameras in a horizontal position. This is effective for panoramic vistas but not usually for faces close-up or sailboats under way.

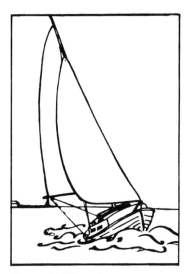

Try vertical formats more often—especially for boats under sail.

Try framing distant scenes with foliage or the frame of a window or doorway. Here, the trunk and overhanging leaves of the tree frame the scene.

the foreground. Don't feel obliged to put a member of the family in the foreground of every picture you take. You'll be less tempted to do this when your actual close-up portraits of the people you love become more powerful.

If funds permit, get something more flexible than a snapshot camera. Most little cameras have such wide-angled lenses (good for close-up group shots) that you'll lack the creative flexibility to photograph faces or distant objects, use filters, or change lenses. I do have one simple camera, a Canon Aquasnappy. It's waterproof! What a handy feature for a sailor, and the pictures it takes have been good enough to publish in national magazines.

If you keep working on your photography, you'll begin to become a slightly different person. You'll begin to really *see.* Your awareness and appreciation for the beauty and interest of the things that surround you may finally lead you to the point where you begin to find the camera an intrusion between yourself and the things beheld. Then, you'll be taking pictures for others, more often than not. As a gift.

When Trouble Comes

I don't intend to teach you to sail. There are a number of good books and videos out there with that sole purpose, and I wouldn't want to leave the impression that sharing tips on certain aspects of sailing safety is sufficient. I urge you to read up on the subject and consider taking a Coast Guard, United States Power Squadron, Canadian Yachting Association, or other water-safety course. To augment that, please mull over the following additional thoughts.

Despite whatever claims about seaworthiness and stability various manufacturers might make for their boats, it is always possible to overturn a small boat. With sufficient bad luck and poor judgment, a driver can turn an *automobile* upside down—so we know what to expect from small boats. The best any manufacturer of small boats can do is design a boat that is difficult to get in trouble with. The rest is up to you. You can at least look for the following:

- **A stable hull design** that lets you move around on deck without dumping you in the drink—and that stoutly resists capsize. The boat can accomplish this with hull shape or with ballast in a keel, or with a combination of the two.
- **A cockpit that self-bails**—that empties itself of water without your having to pump it out. In stormy seas, you'll need your hands to sail the boat. How will you pump if water is slopping over the side?
- **Flotation** that is sufficient for the size and weight of the boat; your boat should not be able to sink out from under you. How long can you and your children tread water? Certainly flotation takes up space, but *under no conditions should you remove it!* You can augment it during a storm by inflating cheap plastic beach balls and wedging them around your cabin. They store flat and can be stuffed into damp, unused crevices the rest of the time.

At great angles of heel, your weight can destabilize the boat—even though it can rescue itself when left to itself.

In addition, you can provide further for your safety by equipping your boat with:

- **Distress flares** and other ways of calling for help (a ship-to-shore radio, an air horn, police whistles, etc.).
- **Flotation devices** for you and your crew (life vests and throwable cushions).
- **An anchor sufficient to hold your boat in high winds** with about 60 feet of line. If you are trying to stop your downwind progress in water too deep for anchoring, you can buy a sea anchor—a cloth cone that drags in the water behind your boat at the end of a line.
- **Whistles and clip-on lights to attach to life vests when cruising at night.** If someone falls overboard in the dark, you can make a recovery.
- **A boarding ladder** so the recovered swimmer can regain the deck. The best kind is the permanent kind mounted to the transom. Single-handed sailors should have no other kind.

ABOUT FOUL WEATHER

First, remember that a small boat is, after all, small. If the weather looks doubtful, it is prudent to stay put—especially if you are coasting along the edge of a large body of water where foul weather could blow you onto a rocky shore, or out to sea. Shelter never looks so precious as it does when it's slipping farther and farther from reach. An effective cockpit enclosure goes a long way to make a small boat livable in foul weather. Stay in port! Then, as the occasional gust of wind makes your whole boat tremble, you can say to yourself, "Boy, I'm sure glad I'm not out in *that!*"

If you are out when conditions threaten, do everything on your safety list at the first sign of trouble. If life jackets can be secured to cockpit enclosure rails or stern pulpits, they can be out of doors *always* and within reach. Often they make good backrests. Get everything you think you'll need out of the cabin at the first sign of a storm so you can secure the hatch and not threaten the boat's watertight integrity by opening up at the height of a storm. If your kids are going to ride out the storm in the cabin, *don't lock them in* or make it impossible for them to get out rapidly should the boat be knocked down.

If you don't wear life jackets in calm weather, get into them quickly if the wind gets up. If you are going to sail in bulky clothing, sweaters, foul weather gear, *always wear your life vest.* You can exhaust yourself rapidly simply trying to stay afloat—and you may be too heavily water-logged for anyone to get you back aboard.

Reduce sail in higher winds, as soon as your boat begins to stagger or feel overpowered. On some boats, a jib can be dropped, in other cases, you'll have to *reef* your mainsail. Reefing is the term for reducing sail area by lowering the sail partially and tying the unused part to the boom. In most cases, the tie-off lines are passed under the sail but *not under the boom.* In reefing, the key is to pull the sail down and out as flat as possible. The following drawings illustrate all the various possibilities there are of reducing sail. Question: When should you reef? Answer: When you first think of it. It's easiest to do it at the dock, otherwise, when you get that first sense of apprehension at the rising wind, go ahead and shorten sail. In stronger winds, your boat will still go fast, and everybody will be safer. There's nothing macho about overstressing your boat and crew—or risking capsize. If you plan on doing more than river and small lake sailing, get reef points put in your sail.

Using Your Outboard. It's a good idea to carry a small jerry can full of gasoline. (I've modified mine by drilling out a hole through the breather cap sufficiently large to squeeze a 1/2-inch plastic hose. With this setup I

Sail reduction strategies.

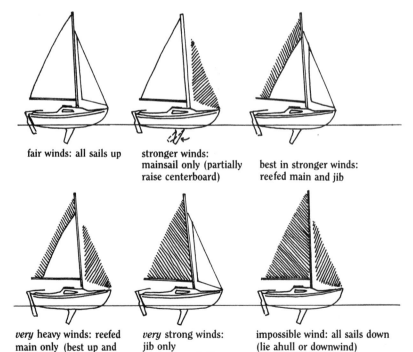

fair winds: all sails up

stronger winds:
mainsail only (partially
raise centerboard)

best in stronger winds:
reefed main and jib

very heavy winds: reefed
main only (best up and
across wind)

very strong winds:
jib only
(best downwind)

impossible wind: all sails down
(lie ahull or downwind)

Here, Fearless *sails reefed down in Lake Kinbasket. Normally the mainsail reaches the masthead.*

can top off my outboard's integral tank without spilling gas into the waters I sail in.) At the first sign of foul weather, top off your outboard's tank, so you won't run out at an awkward moment later. If you've got family or crew with you, discuss in advance who will drop sails and secure the boat, so things can be done smartly when the time comes. Head for shore and safety.

It's safest to motor in storm conditions, if your motor is strong enough to drive you through it. Jib and outboard make an effective storm rig. Tack into the wind as you would under full sail. This helps especially in conditions that overpower your outboard alone.

Centerboard boats benefit by having the centerboard at least part way down while under power. With nothing down, the boat can slide sideways in crosswinds and steer sluggishly. With your board down, your boat will respond smartly and turn on a dime.

Anchoring

Throwing over the hook is a nautical equivalent of setting the parking brake in your car, and the consequences of an abortive anchoring are potentially the same as a brake failure on your car. A lot of technical stuff has been written about anchoring—enough to convince the novice sailor that, like knot-tying and celestial navigation, anchoring is a mystical art requiring years of practice. Not so. On a small boat in normal conditions, you could throw over a line tied to a cinder block and be fine. There are several good reasons why we don't use cinder blocks but, before we get too specific, let's pretend that nothing better had been invented. What if we did anchor to a cinder block? What might happen? We can learn a lot about anchoring by speculating.

> **Situation 1.** There's little wind, slight wave action. The block's weight holds the boat in place nicely. No problem.
> **Situation 2.** The bottom isn't sand or mud, but slate. As a small breeze develops, your cinder block skates along the bottom. You have no grip. Or, conversely, your block wedges itself between two large rocks and, when you want to leave, you can't get the block up again.
> **Situation 3.** Your line is too short or you're trying to anchor in water too deep. There's a slight breeze and some wave action. As each wave passes under your boat, your cinder block is lifted clear of the bottom and, foot by foot, you drift downwind.
> **Situation 4.** During the night, a storm comes up. The block has buried itself snugly into the mud and it's holding, but the boat's up-and-down movement on the waves causes the anchor line to chafe where it's tied around the cinder block's rough edges. Finally, the line is worn through and your boat is free to drift helplessly downwind.

On reflection, we realize that there are three kinds of things to think about when we anchor: We don't want our anchor to drag across the bottom, and we don't want it to be lifted clear by wave action, and we don't want our anchor line chewed in half by friction. A failure in any department will cause us to drift downwind—and maybe go ashore or foul other boats. Let's look briefly at what we can do to ensure against either calamity.

HOLDING THE BOTTOM

There are a number of clever anchor designs that grip the bottom effectively. For a little boat, the Danforth type is probably the best. It holds flat for storage and it offers tremendous holding power for its weight. There are other effective shapes. Many of these, such as the Bruce, are popular on bigger yachts, but the Danforth is less expensive—your best bet.

If you get your anchor tangled in its own line, it won't hold bottom. Don't hurl your anchor into the water; just lower it. That way it won't foul. I've found it best to store the anchor at the bow, tied to the bow pulpit. When sailing alone, or even with company, I run the anchor line through a block at the bow to one of the stern cleats. That way, we can sail or motor into the wind, slow to a stop, and then lower it away without ever leaving the cockpit. Even on a small boat, communicating to some-one standing in the bow is often confusing, and the anchorman blocks your view forward. It can be easier to do it all yourself, unless you're sailing with your kids, in which case, why not designate one of the small hands official anchorman? (In general, find manageable jobs for the kids to do.) Try not to yell when they screw up.

An alternative approach is even simpler: Store the anchor in the cockpit and, after heading into the wind, veer off at the last second and lower the anchor off the stern. Veering off prevents the anchor line from fouling on your rudder or outboard as your line runs out.

Be sure your line is tied to something! I use inexpensive polypropy-lene line. It floats. In the event of carelessness or misunderstanding, at least the line won't sink and the anchor won't be lost forever.

When all is secured, and sails are down and tied, you can decide whether to stay anchored stern-to so the breeze can air out your cabin, or to tie up to your bow cleat—the stronger point of attachment. In a storm, the strongest point of attachment is the bow eye you use to winch your boat onto its trailer. On most small boats, the stern cleats are the least securely attached. Reinforce these with washers or backing pads—or take it easy on them.

KEEPING THE ANCHOR DOWN
This is done simply. Use plenty of line (scope) so that the anchor line pulls at a shallow angle from the bottom. The more line you use, the more elastic the system is and the more effectively the pull on the line digs the flukes of the anchor into the bottom. A length of chain between the anchor and its line dramatically increases holding power. We use a plas-tic-dipped chain. It won't rust, nor will it scratch the surfaces of the boat.

AVOIDING CHAFE
Once you think of chafing, you can instantly think of where to be careful and what to do. Using anchor chain protects from chafe against rocks or coral where your line contacts the bottom. Key knots can be wrapped in

Be sure to let out enough line.

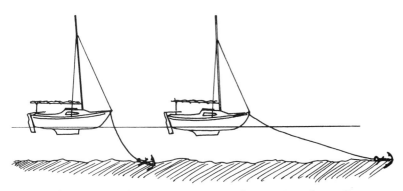

The anchor line is too short. Tension on the line pulls up anchor.

Longer line permits anchor to dig in as tension is applied.

tape or with thin line. Lengths of garden hose are useful too, covering and protecting line where it rubs against the hull or fittings. In a storm, the force of waves slamming against your boat will cause far more stress than the wind itself. The places where the line connects to the hull and to the anchor are the most likely to chafe through.

Check your line periodically for signs of wear. Meanwhile, be reassured that the forces working on a 500- to 1,000-pound sailboat are far more manageable than those working against a 25,000-pound yacht.

KNOW YOUR BOTTOM

A shale or broken slate bottom will prevent your anchor from digging in. Heavy seaweed may plug up things, turning your anchor into a dragging lump of vegetation. A rock bottom may snag your anchor and prevent your getting out again. Here's what's best to do: get into water shallow enough to see the bottom for yourself, then lower away. You can see your anchor to make sure it's clear and well set. If need be, you can jump overboard in shallow water and walk your anchor around to the best spot. With centerboard boats, a falling tide may leave you sitting securely on the bottom—the ideal place to be in a storm. If there are rocks or other debris around, you'll see them before they get you. You can walk ashore. The bigger yachts wouldn't dare come in this close. You can. You'll be safe, you'll have privacy. With 70 feet of line out, you'll be secure against anything.

BEACHING YOUR BOAT

A centerboard boat can pull up right onto a beach and dry out on a falling tide. (If there's no tide, a shoal-keel boat can do it too. If a tide leaves it on its side, it'll be as comfortable as a fun-house in there.) Especially on lakes, provided the bottom is soft sand or mud, why anchor if you can reach the shore and snuggle up for the night? Why indeed? Here are several cautions, however:

In some areas, you may not want to tempt visitors (animal, insect, or human) to walk aboard. The small band of water between you and the shore represents privacy and, in some situations, security.

Secondly, wind-driven waves or the wakes of passing boats can lift your boat into the air, then pound it into the bottom. Keel boats may be

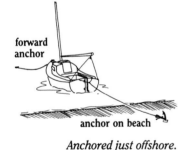

Anchored just offshore.

Left: anchored bow to beach.
Right: anchored stern to beach.

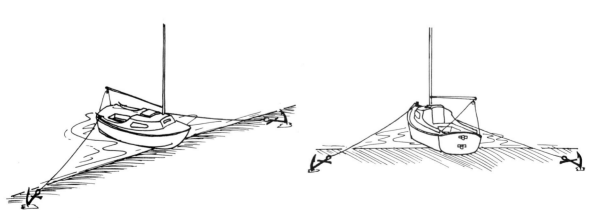

especially vulnerable here. Still, if you have a campsite on the beach or a continual need for access to the beach, physical contact with the beach may be necessary. You'll need two anchors to do it right.

Method 1. Drop your best anchor in deeper water, then back your boat near the beach. Run your second line to the shore and either bury your second anchor on the beach or tie to something handy—such as a tree. When there is wave action, this system is best since you are not touching the bottom and won't be subject to impact or grinding against your hull.

Method 2. Run up your bow on shore and pull up snugly. Run a line off each corner of the stern at a 45 degree angle to the shore so the boat can't drift around and leave you broadside to the beach. Your cockpit faces the water. You have a nice view and some privacy from people on the shore. Should the surf get up though, you'll have waves slamming against the stern. In a severe case, water will pour over the transom into the cockpit and you'll be hammered by inches farther onto the beach. In milder weather, waves may still be noisy and you might have trouble sleeping. If your primary interest is shoreside—perhaps you have your kids camping on the beach—you may want to try Method 3.

Method 3. Remove your rudder so it won't be damaged, then back your boat up onto the beach. Run lines from each side of the bow so the boat will hold its position. Incoming waves will lift the bow and be parted with less noise and impact. It will be easier to get in and out of your boat, plus you'll have a better view of what's going on there. Should the surf get up, you can walk your primary anchor out to deeper water, then pull yourself off into Method 1.

If the shore is rocky or gravelly, stay well clear. Even on windless, waveless days, all it takes is one passing motorboat to lift you up on its wake and slam you down hard on whatever might be there. Find a soft spot on the beach or stay off. In almost any conditions, because you're in a small boat, you can enjoy an intimacy with the shoreline denied larger boats.

CHAPTER 6

The Four Sailing Terrains

THERE ARE ACTUALLY five kinds of places you can go sailing: You can sail on rivers, lakes, bays, along ocean coastlines, or offshore in deep ocean waters. We'll discuss the first four. You can, of course, cross the oceans of the world in a well-equipped small boat, but then you won't be sailing America any more; you'll be sailing the world. That's a whole other subject.

Let's take a look at what you might want to think about when you go out on rivers, lakes, bays, and along the ocean coasts. In each case, there are questions of access, sailing conditions, safety, and comfort. Each kind of sailing has its own charms and demands.

Sailing on Rivers

There are interesting rivers to explore in almost every region of the country. Anyone who's read *Huckleberry Finn* can identify with the romantic idea of loafing down a river, letting the current waft you on your way, and watching the scenery glide by. It's not your most exciting kind of sailing—in fact, you don't want too much excitement in this kind of sailing. River sailing should be low-key, unless you've got a sailing canoe designed for rough water.

ACCESS

Once you've got a river in mind, start with a road atlas and map out a rough outline for your trip. When you have a starting and ending point, phone the police department or the parks and recreation department in the towns where you plan to begin and end your trip. Where are the public launch ramps? Can you park your car and trailer there for a few days? How safe will your car and trailer be while you're gone? Is there any public transportation from your destination back to your starting point so you can return easily to your car? Are there docks or is there a marina where you could tie up your boat in either town? (If there is dockage only at the starting point, you might want to drive your car to your destination and leave it there, taking a bus back.) These are not serious problems, usually, but it helps to have the answers before you start out.

When you launch your boat into a river, remember that there is usually a current. Make sure your boat is well secured and that you have anticipated the boat's intention to begin the voyage immediately, once it's hit the river. It would be embarrassing, to say the least, to be standing on the riverbank watching your boat drift away.

SAILING CONDITIONS

Sailing on rivers often can be frustrating. Tree-lined banks can block much of your wind; you'll often see the leaves on the treetops roiled by breezes that never get to you down on the water. The wind you get often blows either up- or down-channel. A cynic once told me to assume that the wind will be in the direction opposing your course about 75 percent of the time. If the wind is blowing downstream, you may not feel its effect much if the current is also moving you downstream. Sometimes, the wind isn't blowing any faster than the speed of the current. In the Midwest, where the country is flatter, rivers such as the Mississippi may enjoy better winds than some of the Eastern rivers, such as the Connecticut.

In any case, it's advisable to have an effective outboard motor capable of driving you against the current. Otherwise, if you miss your landfall, you won't be able to get upstream to regain it. You'll find the current strongest in the deep center channel. Ride it downstream when you want to make time; pick your way carefully in the shallows if you need to work your way upstream.

Basically, I'd recommend river passages as laid-back sight-seeing excursions. River trips usually are not going to strain your sailing skills; they're good choices for people with a new boat—provided the current is gentle throughout your route. If your river is not a commercial waterway traveled by freighters and tugs, sailing at night can be a romantic treat—especially under a full moon. Here you don't really want to be going too fast anyway. With minimal visibility, you're more apt to bang into things. On the other hand, ghosting down a river at night can be magical. The sounds of dogs barking in the distance and even the soft voices of people talking around a candle on their back patio drift out over the water as you slip downstream. Often, the way ahead seems an impenetrable wall of black until almost the last second, when a shimmering path of reflected starlight appears to one side. Then it's usually the current that takes the boat around anyway. You can't see the sail against the night sky; it's only a black shape breaking the pattern of stars.

Along the East and Gulf coasts, the Intracoastal Waterway provides an inside passage from New York to Texas. We'll discuss the Waterway later but in many ways, river strategies apply to much of the passage. Between inlets, the tide sets up currents that mimic those of rivers—except that the currents reverse directions as the tides ebb and flow. More on that later.

SAFETY

River sailing requires attention to several safety considerations. First of all *you must know for certain that there are no rapids or waterfalls along your route.* Don't just assume this. If there are hydroelectric dams along your river, the dams above or below you could release water to respond to electrical power demands, causing water levels to drop and current to pick up. This can create white-water conditions where you don't expect to find them. You could have the bottom torn out of your boat. If there are power dams along the river you're interested in sailing, the power companies usually will have booklets that offer charts and the locations of ramps and picnic areas. Other sources of information are local boat and canoe dealerships. Be sure you have the reassurance, before you start, that you know what you're getting into.

If you're on a river with commercial barge and freighter traffic, be aware that large vessels *must* stay within a narrow channel or run themselves hard aground. It is the small boat that must stay clear, as the larger boats cannot take evasive action, nor can the larger boats quickly stop if a small boat blunders into their path. Tugboats pulling barges are especially helpless at slow speeds and close quarters. Tugs pulling barges are a special hazard at night. The tow cables are *very* long. Pleasure boats have been known to assume that the tug and the tow were two separate vessels in fog or darkness. Thinking to sail between them, sailboats have fouled their rigging in the cable, lost their masts, and then been trampled under by the barge in tow. Stay well clear of commercial boats.

If you pull onto a beach facing water traveled by large commercial boats, be alert that their wakes can wreak havoc along the shoreline. From a distance, they may appear to be slipping easily along, throwing little wake. The problem is that they are displacing so much water in a narrow channel that while they are making only small waves, they are dragging a huge amount of water along with them. Once, along the entrance to the Cape Cod Canal, we saw a passing freighter create such a powerful surge that a half-dozen beached motorboats and several swimmers were hurled 50 yards up the beach. If commercial traffic is apt to pass, anchor in hip-deep water with at least 50 feet of line, rather than beach the boat. If swimmers are on the beach, especially little children, have them get at least 10 yards above the water's edge when freighters go by—at least for the first time one goes by—so you'll know what effect it has. Repeat that precaution on every beach you visit since bottom conditions change continually on a river. This precaution is especially important at night. In quiet, untrafficked waters, you often can tie to trees along the riverbank. If swept by a heavy freighter, your boat could be dashed into the riverbank or dismasted as it's swept into overhanging trees. I've traveled without any problems along several waterways trafficked by barges and freighters, but precaution is still in order. If you can find a little creek or backwater in which to anchor for the night, you'll have done well. These concerns are equally applicable to sailing and motoring along the Intracoastal Waterway or in canals.

There are other, smaller things bobbing downriver worth your notice. Logs, brush, 55-gallon drums, all sorts of things are accompanying you downstream. Keep an eye out, if you're motoring especially, not to foul your prop or bang into things. If you're sailing with children, they can take turns mounting watch at the bow if you've seen any evidence of floating debris. Beware also, if ocean sailing offshore, that the mouths of large rivers will be discharging all manner of trash.

Especially in rivers and canals, beware of commercial traffic. The wakes *as well as the vessels themselves can do real damage.*

Rivers also can carry trash of an altogether different sort. Cities and rural towns are not above flushing their collective toilets into scenic waterways. Rivers such as the St. Lawrence are not only heavily trafficked by freighters and tankers (many of whom leave oil slicks behind them) but have factories and processing plants dotted along their banks—foul things, these. Agricultural runoff, fertilizers especially, also flows into the waterways.

An area favored by nude bathers once spread along a twenty mile stretch of the Connecticut River in New Hampshire and Vermont. Just downstream, a town was discharging sewage effuent into the river. A public outcry closed the bathers down, but no comparable civic righteousness shut off the overflowing sewage. Since we're part of a culture that is still more embarrassed by our bodies than by the things that poison them, you, dear sailor, will have to take care where you swim while you're sailing America.

The same sources of information that advise you of other conditions can advise you also about local water cleanliness: power companies, state, federal, and provincial fish and game departments, parks and recreational departments, marinas, and boat dealerships. If you have any doubts, it's good to bring along an extra jerry can of water to sprinkle down with after swimming—and tell the kids not to drink the water.

And if you have doubts about drinking the water, extend them to eating any fish you might catch. Areas near mines, for example, are often contaminated by runoff. We found this to be true in some Western lakes, which had high mercury levels. Pregnant women should be especially cautious.

Finally, if swimming from a beach or an anchored boat, warn children to stay close if the river's current is capable of washing them out of reach. On a lazy day, you can drift on down the river with a bunch of inner tubes floating on the ends of lines. Kids can have a ball this way and it's safe enough, so long as the adults keep an eye on things.

As before, do not allow my suggested precautions to deter you from riverboating. There are rivers in this country and elsewhere that tempt me still. Rivers can be a special pleasure for the small-boat navigator. They require no more (or less) prudence than anything else you do on a small boat.

Sailing on Lakes

ACCESS

There basically are two kinds of lakes: natural and man-made. In general, lakes pose fewer access problems than do rivers, since it's so much easier to return to your starting point. Most popular lakes have at least a couple of launching facilities. Your ease of access will depend on the local politics. Some smaller lakes are controlled by owners' associations—the people who own the properties surrounding the lake. In New Hampshire, for example, there are restrictive ordinances controlling registration, launching, use of outboard motors, and sleeping on board overnight. In the defense of such organizations, one can understand the reluctance of beachfront owners to see their lakes turn into noisy, littered, and congested playgrounds for strangers. On the other hand, unrestricted freedom of property owners to turn our waterways onto privileged preserves will introduce a mean-spiritedness to public recreation that has no place in North America. Fortunately, access is not a pervasive problem, and that's good; lakes are the ideal proving ground for new sailors to learn how to get around in small boats.

Man-made lakes usually have been designed as multipurpose facilities. Often the dams that form such lakes provide hydroelectric power. The lakes themselves can serve as reservoirs for cities and farms. Usually, the power companies (or the Army Corps of Engineers) who completed the project have provided excellent parking, launching, and camping facilities—making man-made lakes ideal vacation spots. Since the land around such lakes is often publicly or corporately owned, there is usually more wilderness scenery as well as more access to the shoreline.

North America is laced with tens of thousands of lakes. Even rivers occasionally widen into open lake areas. The St. Lawrence does this (Lac St. Pierre) as does the Mississippi (Lake Pontchartrain). If you're new to sailing, the lakes are a natural first step.

SAILING CONDITIONS

Small inland lakes do not have enough mass to create their own weather, so they'll be apt to share in whatever weather the local region offers. Winds can be light and irregular in some lakes. In flat country blessed with an almost constant wind, you'll get superb conditions. If mountains shelter long, skinny lakes, the breezes are apt to blow either up or down the length of the lake. Once a friend took me out on his Com-pac 16 and we found winds so confused that the masthead wind indicator spun like a top. If you can learn to sail in a lake, you'll actually find sailing a snap on larger bodies of water where the winds are steadier.

Many lakes, especially man-made ones, have rocky shorelines; you'll have to approach the shoreline with caution until you've got the place figured out. The water in most public lakes is fairly clean. You'll want to have a marine toilet of some kind aboard so that you don't foul the place up. There are usually heavy fines for dumping sewage into public waterways—as there should be.

SAFETY

On the whole, lake sailing is the safest kind of sailing. Still, there are things to watch. Some inland lakes, for example, are crossed by power lines. Catamarans, or other boats with tall masts, have been known to foul power lines, electrocuting the crew. **In launching too, beware of overhead wires!** They can kill you or a member of your family. It happens almost every year.

Keep a lookout for whatever might be floating on the surface. Mountain lakes or lakes surrounded by forest may have logs and stumps floating almost completely submerged. Most at risk are motorboats and fast catamarans, zooming along flying one hull. Motorboats themselves bear watching. For many boaters, time on the water is the occasion for continuous drinking. A drunk in a high-powered boat is not your ideal neighbor out on a lake.

If your lake is glacially fed, or fed by snow melt, the water's going to be very cold. Even in August, a capsize can become a serious matter if you can't get the boat upright and get your crew out of the water in about 15 minutes. The colder the water, the less time you have before hypothermia leaches away body heat. The Great Lakes combine cold water and oceanic sea conditions, and therefore deserve great respect.

While weather on most small to moderately sized lakes is usually mild, watch out for thunderstorms. Remember that inland lakes are subject to inland weather. Have a chain with a shackle on one end that you can clip to one of the wire stays—thereby electrically grounding your boat should lightning strike your mast. Without a grounding connection, lightning makes its own weird path to the water. Since human beings are more than 80 percent water, we make an attractive path of least resistance. Lightning, unassisted by a grounding cable, has been known to pass through sailors in its path from the mast to the sea. Finally, moderately sized lakes can kick up a nasty chop in storms. Seek shelter if a thunderstorm seems imminent. If caught out, lower the sail, clip on your ground-chain, and pick a soft stretch of shoreline downwind. Let your family find shelter below away from the mast or, in an open boat, use the sail like a tarp to shelter people from the rain while your boat drifts to shore. No safe shelter ashore? Stay put and dry on your boat, under the sail. Thunderstorms don't last long.

All things considered, lakes provide your safest and most accessible sailing. The largest lakes are too big to see across. You can work your way up to serious oceanic sailing in North America without ever venturing onto salt water.

Sailing in Gulfs and Bays

ACCESS

Now we're getting into the big time. In the continent's gulfs and bays, we get tidal waters that add interesting currents. Tides also continually change the water's depth along the shoreline, making both anchoring and navigation more challenging. Beached sailboats that are not otherwise fixed to the shoreline can be floated off by a rising tide, or rocks can slowly emerge from the water with a falling tide to bang the underside of your boat. Your boat can be grounded by a falling tide, if you leave it unattended on a beach or too close to shore.

Tides, currents, and longer fetch for waves to develop combine to make bay and gulf sailing both demanding and exciting. If you're planning a trip to such an area, write to local chambers of commerce, time permitting, for information. You can pick a likely starting spot and call the local police or parks and recreation department for information on good ramps and parking, or the names of nearby marinas. If you need a deep ramp to launch your boat, be sure to inquire about that. Remember too that some ramps are excellent at high tide and almost useless at low tide.

If you can plan your vacation so that you're using shoreside facilities on weekdays, you'll avoid lots of congestion. Places will seem more scenic.

Bay sailing opens up the possibility of real voyaging. A Montgomery 15 sails in Long Island Sound.

SAILING CONDITIONS

The winds on the country's gulfs and bays are apt to be steadier (and often stronger) than they are on most lakes. This makes sailing fun. You can often lay a course and keep to it all day long. Generally, summer winds will be lighter in the morning, then build during the afternoon. Things get quieter in the late afternoon, usually, and then a light wind will often blow most of the night. In most cases, the solar heating of the mainland powers onshore winds all day and lighter offshore breezes at night. When winds blow for a period of time over large bodies of water, waves get impressive. This can add to the excitement, especially for inland sailors used to flat water.

There's another aspect to saltwater sailing—the salt. Salt water does unhappy things to metals, including outboards and trailers. When you return home, fill a trash can with the garden hose. Stick your motor in it and let it run for a few minutes. Then hose down the trailer carefully. A used outboard motor is a better buy if it's been used on a freshwater lake than if it's spent its life in salt water.

Since salt retains moisture, you'll get a clammy feeling if you go swimming and don't wash the dried salt off your body. Clothing wet with salt water will seem to dry but will absorb humidity. So will sheets and bedding. Have a set of rough-and-ready clothes that you can wear during the most active part of your sailing day. When evening comes, sponge off with fresh water and change into fresh clothes reserved just for the purpose. You'll feel good that way. Make a rule to reserve whatever you use for pajamas for sleeping only, so they'll always be dry. Pull a trash bag over the aft end of your mattresses during the day if people are going to be changing out of wet bathing suits in the cabin. Salt water sounds serious and romantic to the freshwater sailor, but it's actually a nuisance.

SAFETY

If you're making a nighttime passage, be sure you've got recent marine charts and that you understand the system of red, green, and white flashing lights that mark nautical routes. Make sure you have proper lights on your boat and that you can visualize and understand the lights other vessels carry. There are several good books on sailing lore that illustrate and explain these things well. If unsure of either your skills or the waters, try making an hour's loop out and back from your evening's berth. Enjoy the ambiance of nighttime sailing; see how things look. Don't try a night passage if your skills aren't sharpened by some experience.

Remember too that the channels marked by lighted buoys will be used by other vessels—maybe even full-sized freighters or by tugs with barges in tow. Commercial boats cannot maneuver or even come to a stop rapidly, nor can they easily see small boats close to the water. Their equipment is designed to prevent their colliding with other vessels their size. Be careful. Moonlit nights are best. Not only is visibility much improved (weather cooperating) but it's so beautiful you'll hardly be able to stand it.

You'll need to know if fog is common in the area. You'll need to have a compass. If fog rolls in, don't panic. Note your course, note which direction the waves are coming from, and get your bearings. Get a compass heading for your destination. Then relax and enjoy something weird. Once you're socked in, you'll note that the waves are coming from the same direction as they were previously. That, along with your compass, will help you. Turn off your motor so you can hear things you shouldn't miss. Oh yes, are there any currents that might set you off course? Estimate a little compensation.

Tides and tidal currents not only can add interest and excitement to saltwater sailing, but an element of risk. Tide can carry an incapacitated boat out to sea, for example. When wind and tidal currents blow and flow in opposite directions—especially in fairly shallow water—waves can get very steep and close together. Get a tide table, a marine chart, and a weather radio (Radio Shack has some good, cheap ones). Plot your route in advance, checking the tides and expected winds. You're learning another set of skills; as we said, bay and gulf sailing is getting into the big-time league. You cannot approach it with the casualness you have when you drop your boat into the local lake—but then the rewards in pride and adventure are different too.

Coastal Sailing

ACCESS

A glance at a highway map suggests the possibilities for sailing along the nation's coastlines. Now you're in the ocean! What you need now are seaports. Many of these are famous; others will only show up in marine charts. I'd suggest you buy one of the regional cruising guides to best preview what the areas offer. (See "Useful Books and Videos" in the Appendices.) Otherwise, everything covered in "Bays and Gulfs" applies here too.

SAILING CONDITIONS

Expect winds to be comparable with what we've discussed in the previous section. You'll have tides and currents here too, of course. When sailing along coasts, you have access considerations of a different sort: when you want to stop sailing along the coastline, you need an inlet to return to protected waters. As tides funnel large volumes of water into and out of these inlets, currents can be very strong. If winds are onshore while the tide is running hard out to sea, huge seas can develop at the inlet's mouth. Be careful! More of this later. You need to have inlets strung out in convenient places too. The Pacific coast has relatively few ports. If caught between harbors in a coastal passage, you'll have to be sufficiently seaworthy to stay out in foul weather.

In some cases offshore islands beckon, such as Catalina Island about 26 miles offshore from Marina del Rey, California. Large waves by themselves are not hazardous—and you'll get some full ocean swells, sailing the coasts. But when large waves get into shallow water, they become unstable and break. Breaking seas are big, fast, and very heavy. They can sweep your boat clear, tear off sails, break spars, roll her over, fill her with water, and carry away you or your crew. You must know what you're doing and where you are. Sandbars well offshore can cause seas to break. If you sail too close to shore, it will be the unusually big wave that feels the bottom when the others don't—and breaks. The one that gets you will be the biggest one. Be conservative and stay well off except on the mildest days. At least if you're near shore in shallow water, your boat will be bowled over in sight of shore. You'll likely be washed onto the beach, soggy and embarrassed, to the amusement of sunbathers.

Winds are usually onshore by day, offshore by night. Get a weather radio and stay advised. Powerful winds can either blow you onto shore or, maybe worse, out to sea. And we said earlier that offshore sailing was not what we had in mind.

SAFETY

The major hazards have already been suggested: Avoid breaking seas; look out for strong currents and winds; and know where you are at all times so you're mindful of underwater hazards. How can you best see to all this?

Plan to run inlets at slack water, when the tide is running hard neither in nor out. Find out about the inlets you plan to run by checking a waterway guide or by asking around. In a pinch, you can phone a local coast guard station to ask if there's anything you ought to know. Small boats often have neither room nor budget for depth sounders, but larger boats use them frequently when approaching shore. Even in a fog, a navigator with a depth sounder and a chart can follow a contour of depth along the shoreline until the channel to shelter leads him in.

Get official marine charts for the waters in which you plan to sail. Coastal cruising guides help too. Look over the charts before you sail to get an overall idea of what's ahead.

Have good anchors and lots of line in good condition. If you're being blown ashore against your will, the anchor will be your last resort. In addition, a drogue (sea anchor) can be useful. Sea anchors are stout canvas cones that drag in the water behind your boat to keep you from being blown too rapidly downwind in water too deep for conventional anchoring.

Your boat should be rigged solidly with all stressed fittings (including cleats) backed up so they can't tear from the deck. You do not want a rigging failure at sea. You too should be ready for ocean sailing. Work your way up to it.

Have a weather radio and be reassured that storms or hazardous conditions are not developing. A ship-to-shore radio gives you a way to ask for advice or assistance. As a last resort, an EPIRB rescue beacon can signal your need for rescue to satellites that will pinpoint your location and relay your distress call. For local stuff, of course you'll have a flare pistol.

Here's a tip you can use on all large bodies of water. If a storm is approaching and you don't know where the harbors are, check around for other boats. If they're running for cover, watch where in the shoreline they seem to be disappearing. Then follow them. Don't wait till you're all alone before looking around.

We have an almost instinctive attraction to water. We want to go sailing; we'll pay big bucks to tear a lobster apart next to an ocean view. But since we can neither breathe water nor walk upon it, we must be always prudent, always watchful.

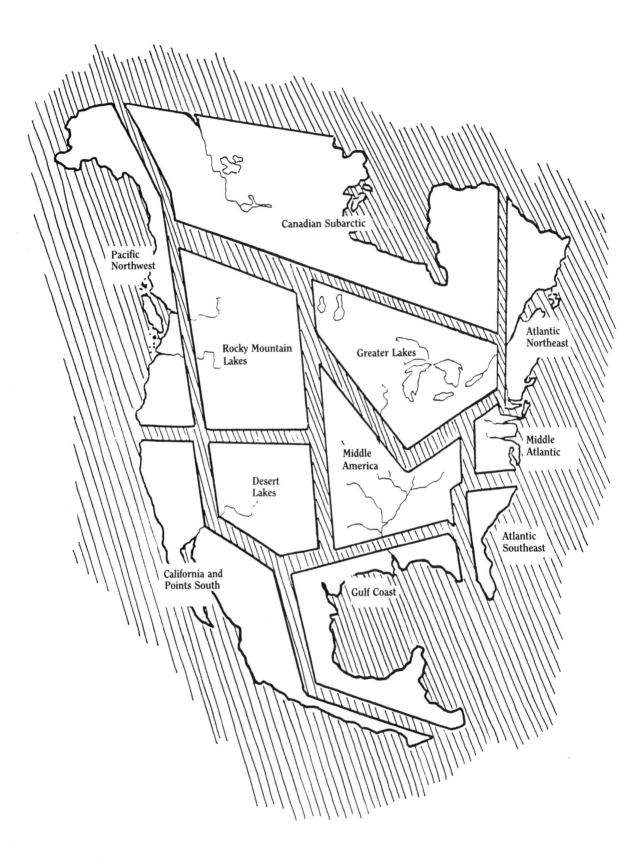

An Introductory Note

We have traveled to and sailed in places all around the continent. Our adventures, literally boxes and boxes of literature from various states and Canadian provinces, and the first-hand experiences of dozens of sailors from around the country I've collected over 10 years from articles in *Sail, Cruising World,* and *Small Boat Journal* provide the foundation for this section.

What follows is an overview of each region and its principal delights. These are often the same places preferred by big-boat sailors, but not necessarily. Trailer sailors can, for example, easily drive around canals that deepwater boats must traverse, and they can sneak into shallows off limits to bigger boats. On the other hand, they may find it prudent to avoid places that deeper and more powerful boats can go. Large sailboats with more powerful motors can run upriver against the current, a difficult task for small boats. Consequently, I devote less space in this section to rivers than will a cruising guide for larger boats. Smaller boats can launch more easily upriver, run downstream with the current, and emerge in a larger body of water. But then there's the hassle of finding a way to return for car and trailer. All these sorts of variables entered into deciding what to mention and how much detail to supply.

A continental review such as this cannot serve as an alternative for local charts and more detailed information. But it does give you something that's been missing until now: a broad sweeping look at North America as a whole so you can form useful impressions and get started gathering information on places that interest you.

Before we begin, let's establish a way of classifying each place we discuss according to the degree of experience required to negotiate it safely. No area is entirely free of hazards, so this system is a relative sort of thing:

novice. A reasonable location for someone who is new to sailing.

mariner. Requires the kind of experience usually gained after several summers of lake and (some) bay sailing.

expert. Fog, currents, rocks, or sea conditions demand a seasoned sailor and a vessel equipped for rugged conditions.

adventurer. Combines levels of risk or discomfort that would discourage anyone not seeking these things and prepared to accept the consequences.

When we set out on our 10,000-mile circuit of the continent, we had little to go by—just a road atlas, a good car, and a good boat. We rolled down the window a lot and asked questions. It was fun and, knowing all I do now, I don't think I'd have changed the route at all. We were lucky. With this book, I hope you'll be able to take trips in your mind before you hop in your car.

PART
II

A Trailer Sailor's Trip Guide to North America

CHAPTER 7

The Atlantic Northeast

QUEBEC

St. Lawrence River

Gaspé

17 Gulf of St. Lawrence

Tadoussac

Charlottetown
(Prince Edward Island)

NEW BRUNSWICK

NOVA
SCOTIA

16

Quebec

Fredericton

QUEBEC

MAINE

St. John

Halifax

14

15

Montreal

Bangor

Yarmouth

Atlantic Ocean

13

Penobscot River

VERMONT

Augusta

12

Kennebec River

10

11

Portland

NEW
HAMPSHIRE

Connecticut River

Boston

Plymouth

MASSACHUSETTS

9

Cape Cod

Hartford

4

5

7

CONNECTICUT

0

8

New Haven

1 2 3

6

RHODE ISLAND

Points of Interest

1. Saybrook
2. Mystic
3. Block Island
4. Narragansett Bay
5. Buzzards Bay
6. Martha's Vineyard
7. Nantucket Sound
8. Nantucket
9. Cape Cod Bay
10. Lake Winnipesaukee
11. Casco Bay
12. Penobscot Bay
13. Acadia National Park
14. Passamaquoddy Bay
15. Bay of Fundy
16. Bras d'Or Lake
17. Perce Rock

Approximate Miles

0   100   200   300

THIS AREA INCLUDES the Canadian provinces of Quebec, New Brunswick, Prince Edward Island, and Nova Scotia, and the states of Maine, New Hampshire, Vermont, Massachusetts, Rhode Island, and Connecticut. Traditionally, New England is one of the places most people associate with yachting. But for both Canada and the U.S., this is an area of early settlement and the sea is only one of its traditions. There's a lot of history here. It was because of the nature of the Northeastern coastline that sailing established itself so early. The shoreline, be it rocky or sandy, is laced with natural harbors and bays. The abundance of fish and shellfish created an economic incentive for many people to take to the sea in small boats. People immigrated here from seafaring places too: Scotland, Ireland, England, and Portugal. A rich tradition of small boating developed that, in time, was joined by a yachting interest.

The coastal sailing opportunities of the Atlantic Northeast are matched by inland opportunities. The region is dotted with glacially-carved lakes and cut by two navigable rivers, the Connecticut and the mighty St. Lawrence. Visits to any of these attractions take you through historical countryside and, especially along the ocean coast, invite you to sample what may be the Western world's finest seafood cuisine.

Rivers of the Atlantic Northeast

THE CONNECTICUT

The Connecticut River has its source near the Canadian border. It is nourished in springtime with the snow melt from much of New England's mountain system and its northern portions can become loud and fast. A series of dams has been set up to harness the Connecticut's power, and navigating the river from source to mouth is not possible without portaging or trailering around several dams.

There is surprisingly little industrial or urban development along the Connecticut. Passages on the upper river, while not especially breezy or exciting, are beautifully pastoral. The river tends to shoal as you head north and approach each dam. For obvious safety reasons, you should obtain information on the exact whereabouts of each dam before you set out. You also need to have an outboard motor capable of driving your boat against a 4- to 5-knot current. It rarely reaches that strength, but in places where the current picks up, you'll need the extra power.

The Connecticut is a fairly clean river, as Eastern rivers go. Be aware that farming produces its own kinds of pollution, and a few towns may still dump raw effluent into the river. I would not recommend the area 20 miles south of Hartford for swimming. When we've been on the river, we've used this very unscientific rule of thumb: When the river water, closely observed, gives us no obvious reason to be concerned, we go swimming. We do *not* drink the water and we rinse off after swimming with tap water brought along for that purpose.

The Connecticut River is a **novice class** location. I'm not implying that only a beginner would enjoy the place, just that an old salt would not be stressed or stretched by it.

THE ST. LAWRENCE

The St. Lawrence is the mightiest river system on the East Coast, rumbling northeast to the Atlantic from the Great Lakes. For the small-boat sailor, its source at Lake Ontario is a fascinating maze of channels dotting the Thousand Islands region, a gunkholer's paradise. The water is sheltered; there are countless places of interest to visit, and you don't have to go very far to have a good time. It's an ideal **novice** location—and an excellent choice for a family with small children, since there are no long passages under sail.

At Montreal, first settled by the French in 1642, the St. Lawrence is interrupted by the mighty Lachine Rapids, which would crush a small, misdirected boat. It was these rapids, in fact, that stymied the French expansion upstream. Heading down the St. Lawrence near Lachine, know where you are at all times; there is a system of locks and canals around the rapids.

Some 180 miles downstream to the northeast is Quebec City, established by the French as a trading post in 1608. You can put in north of Montreal and sail with the current to Quebec City without too much trouble. About halfway between the two cities, near Trois Rivieres, Lac Saint-Pierre opens the river up for a 20-mile stretch. The water in the lake is shallow, and high winds can whip up nasty conditions. When we sailed our little Potter there, northwest winds rose to 35 to 40 knots. The lake rapidly emptied itself of boats and we were forced to reach across the lake in what were, for a little boat, survival conditions. We did the 20-mile crossing in three and a half hours at 6½ knots on bare poles, all sails down. Although big seas threatened to break over the stern and swamp the boat, none of them actually made it in. We arrived dry and safe, but badly shaken.

About 20 miles north of the lake, standing waves occasionally form in the river. Consult marine charts; sneaking around such a problem in the shallows near the river's edge, where the current isn't as swift and where you can drop anchor quickly, may be the best solution.

The Château Frontenac stands vigil over the St. Lawrence. Courtesy of Tourisme Québec.

Quebec City is a beautiful place—the only walled city in North America. You'll need a powerful motor here as the current is swift. With insufficient motor power, you could be swept right past the city.

In the lower river, the banks and bottom are mostly sand and mud. As you go north, the coast becomes more rocky. North of Quebec City, the river begins to open up dramatically into the Gulf of St. Lawrence.

Just north of Quebec is the Island of Orleans, a vision of the French countryside well worth visiting. In the fall the apples here are delicious and *huge*—almost a meal in themselves.

The farther north you go, the more the gulf opens. Tides increase in strength and influence; the water becomes more salty. The spectacular but fast-moving Saguenay River joins the St. Lawrence at Tadoussac, where thousand-foot cliffs abruptly meet the water. Where the river between Montreal and Quebec calls for a **mariner** with some experience, the gulf calls for an **expert** seaman. The scenery is spectacular and rewarding, but the conditions are demanding, and the cold waters of the northern gulf combined with its rugged shoreline would exact dear payment for mistakes or bad luck.

The St. Lawrence is cursed with serious pollution from Montreal north to the Saguenay. Beluga whales have washed ashore at Tadoussac so riddled with industrial pollutants that the carcasses themselves required disposal as toxic wastes. Swimming in the Thousand Islands is good, but my family declined to swim in any of the waters north of Montreal on our trip there a few years ago. I'd like to think it's better now, but I'm not convinced it is.

SOME INTERESTING RIVERS DOWN EAST

There are several beautiful rivers in Maine and New Brunswick that take you into the interior from the Atlantic, Penobscot Bay, and the Bay of Fundy. Larger sailboats (with auxiliary engines more powerful than you'll find on most little sailboats) relish the scenery and the small towns along the river runs, but you'll be doing it the hard way if you start downriver in the bays and try to motor upstream. If a combination river and bay trip

Where the Gulf of St. Lawrence empties out into the Atlantic you'll find the Perce Rock at Gaspé. What a spectacular place to bring a small boat. Courtesy of Tourisme Québec.

appeals to you, launch upriver and glide down with the current. After sailing around in whatever bay you reach, tie up at one of the larger towns, and hitchhike or take a bus back to your starting point to retrieve your car and trailer. Because of the powerful tides and the rocky terrain, I'd rate all of these as **mariner** class sailing grounds.

If time is limited, Maine's Casco and Penobscot bays have sheltered as well as open sailing areas, and you might just limit your river explorations to the rivers' mouths—letting a rising tide boost you in a bit.

The Piscataqua River separates Portsmouth, New Hampshire and Kittery, Maine at its mouth. Upriver a bit, an arm of the river forms Great Bay, an additional point of interest.

The Kennebec River and the Damariscotta River empty into the Atlantic east of Casco Bay. Protected little bays carved by Ice Age glaciers protect the mouth of the Kennebec and the town of Bath, once the builder of many of the great multimasted schooners that graced the last days of working sail. The Kennebec is navigable at least 40 miles—all the way to Augusta.

The Damariscotta River is very pretty too. You pass the town of Damariscotta up to an arm of the river called Damariscotta Lake, where you can find, not too surprisingly, Damariscotta Lake State Park. There are strong currents above the town; it's best to put in at the state park and work your way downstream from the lake.

The Penobscot River flows into the bay of the same name. Belfast and Searsport lie at the head of the bay. The scenery is beautiful, and you can navigate the river all the way to Bangor in a small boat.

The St. John River in New Brunswick, with the port of St. John at its mouth, is a cruising ground unto itself. Inland, the river branches into several long "lakes," the largest of which is Grand Lake. You can navigate to (or from) Fredericton. Since the Bay of Fundy can be more than I'd recommend for most small-boat sailors not raised in these parts, the St. John cruising ground might be the finest way to get to know the area.

Sailing America: Pottering on the Connecticut

"Believe me, my young friend, there is *nothing,* absolutely nothing, half so much worth doing as simply messing about in boats. Whether you get away, or whether you don't; whether you arrive at your destination, or whether you reach somewhere else; whether you never get anywhere at all, you're always busy, and you never do anything in particular. And when you're done there's always something else."

Thus spoke the Water Rat to his friend Mole, inviting him to a day on the river. This invitation had its own appeal to us a few years back having come to Vermont from the sea. We had shed our bigger boat in favor of *Fearless,* a little Potter 15. In one summer *Fearless* had taken us to the St. Lawrence River, Lake Champlain, Buzzards Bay, and the sea. Small can be beautiful.

The Connecticut River begins in northern New Hampshire and winds more than 400 miles through four New England states on its route to Long Island Sound. Over the years, the river has been sectioned by a grid of power dams. Now it's easier to think of it as a salami string of lakes whose levels and currents are controlled by the engineers of Northeast Utilities. To get a feeling for the river as a whole, we selected three sections—an upper, a middle, and a lower and began, in no particular order, to go exploring.

First up was the section of the river most familiar to yachtsmen, the final leg from Hartford to the Sound. Needing a midsummer vacation from the kids, Bettina and I decided to do this one alone. Wethersfield Cove, just a few miles south of Hartford, was an ideal put-in place for small boats. An immense ramp almost 100 yards wide got us afloat easily. There was generous space for parking too, well patrolled at night. Bettina rigged the boat while I put the car to bed and we were off—out of the cove, under the rumble of I-91, and into the river. An indifferent wind and a subtle, but insistent, current urged us gently down toward the sea.

What little there was left of Hartford soon vanished and we glided past woods and plowed fields. There were few houses anywhere along the river; we were amazed how "away from it all" we felt. Soon, though, it was past five and Hartford, tired of mechanized labor, turned to mechanized recreation. Soon the woods along the riverbank buzzed like a nest of hornets as unseen motor-cycles prowled the back roads. Motorboats appeared dragging waterskiers up and down the river. For an hour or so, the Connecticut became a dragstrip. Then the activity gradually abated; the sun dropped. We took our first swim, then set up our cockpit kitchen for dinner. Soon it was dark. The moon rose and we had the blue propane flame of our one-burner stove. When we shut off the hiss of the stove, the silence rushed in. Occasionally, through the trees, a light would drift by—an illuminated back porch, a dog barking, the soft murmur of conversation. At times the river ahead would seem a wall of impenetrable black; then the faint outline of a pathway would emerge and we would ripple on. Though we had a faint breeze to help us on our way, we thought of Mark Twain's recollected navigations on the nighttime Mississippi.

Finally we were too tired to continue. Ahead we could see the lights of the Middletown bridge. After such a night, civilization was too much to bear. We pulled over to the riverbank and, soothed by what sounded like a small waterfall, we turned in.

We woke to find the water around us fouled with debris and an oily brown scum. Our romantic waterfall of the night before had suddenly lost its allure as an endless supply of effluent drifted by. So much for our wake-up plunge. We shoved off, coasted under the bridge, and ate our breakfast underway. More countryside slipped by, the water gradually cleared and slowly the works of man started to appear.

Hydro isn't the only power to operate along the Connecticut; nuclear is there also, needing the river for a continuous flow of coolant. As we approached our first nuclear facility, we noticed a large black box, suspended on a tripod, standing on the riverbank. Mildly curious, we fired up our little one-horsepower Elliott and headed over for a look. But the wind died, the current picked up, and we finally swung off and continued past the plant. Downstream, we noticed another tripod and box and threw over the helm, determined this time to have a look. Then, a Boston Whaler with "U.S. Army" on its sides appeared carrying a fellow in a flowered shirt. He sped past us, landed on the shore, and removed the black box from its tripod. He sped by us again with the box resting on the floor of the boat. We waved hello; he waved back. We still wonder what that was all about. Just paranoid, I guess.

Below the Haddam bridge, the river widened and the scenery grew more interesting. We beached and visited a castle built by William Gillette, the actor who immortalized Sherlock Holmes on stage around the turn of the century.

Gillette erected his oddity after the death of his young and very beautiful wife. The Taj Mahal was a tomb for the wife of a prince; Gillette seems to have built this place as a tomb for himself. The castle had a Disneyland quality to it, built as it was, so obviously for effect and not for function. From its clifftop, the castle offers breathtaking views of the river, and ice cream—a delicious break from the rigors of small boat cruising. But as we walked around and saw the narrow single beds in the tiny bedrooms Gillette had built for himself, we could imagine this perpetually grief-stricken man wandering the halls at night searching for a place to rest. That was sad.

Farther downriver we pulled over to get a better look at a strange sight. The upturned hull of a wooden boat hung in a tree back from the riverbank. A sandy beach ran into the woods littered here and there with torn sheets of plywood and fragments of furniture. The spring flood that had caused such havoc upriver had obviously extended farther south than we had imagined. From our normal, comfortable spot near the beach we looked again at the hull twenty feet over our heads and hoped for the sake of those living along the river that waters would never rise high enough to sweep those remains downstream again.

We ended the second day at Essex, planning simply to pull the boat up onto the beach on Essex Island. But we learned that the island was a private, floating condominium, and instead tied up to a piling at the town wharf and were treated to a concert of traditional Irish and maritime songs by a smashing group, The Morgans, from Mystic. Then we wandered into town and blew a third of our cruise budget on dinner.

When we returned to the dock, we found we were next to a young couple on a San Juan 21. We visited awhile, shared a beer, a look at a local chart, and some good conversation. They were in the market for a bigger boat. The interior of the 21, which seemed a palace compared with the cabin of our Potter, was "too small" and, moreover, the 21-footer made them afraid. A bigger boat, possibly a deep-keel boat, they thought, might give them a greater sense of security. Later, Tina and I shook our heads. These bright and friendly people hadn't begun to exhaust the potential of the boat they already had. Their boat was aging but still perfectly sound and ready for improvements. Yet they were all set to go into hock and trade up. It's good business, I guess. Still, there's much to be said for going small, for owning it outright. It's a shame, but we continually meet people who own much bigger boats yet do far less than we do in little *Fearless*.

Day three saw fickle winds. The last few miles of the Connecticut are a mariner's paradise, with sandy beaches for an early morning swim and a shave, big marinas for dockage and repairs, and an entrance into Long Island Sound free of urban sprawl and blight. The Connecticut has no city at its mouth. As we rounded up north into the Sound, the wind died, leaving us at the mercy of the powerboats whose wakes continually roiled the waters. Most offensive were the long muscle boats, whose throaty exhausts bellowed like stratofortresses as they plied the coast. Their noise reached us before they could be seen and lingered on after they were gone from sight. It was hot and muggy; we rolled and drifted sluggishly under a white sky. We had a crummy afternoon of it. Finally we reached the cove of Niantic. Here and in every inland pocket, the wind was delightful. We rushed along joyfully until we got to the northern extremity of the cove, where the wind died and we stopped in our tracks. Disgusted, we fired up the Power Paddle and headed in, picked up the wind, and boiled in to the Niantic Yacht Club with a bone in our teeth. The hospitality there couldn't have been more gracious. We got showers, a mooring, and a trip into town. We gorged on seafood at King Neptune's Fish Market. Their bluefish cheeks, a hard-to-find delicacy, were excellent, as was their chowder and lobster. We returned to bed cooled, stuffed, and refreshed.

Our final day saw more white sky, lousy wind, and sloppy seas. The deep mouth of the Thames had wind and we cut a curving swath through the port, then drifted to the mouth of the Mystic River, where a fresh wind bore us into that historic port and to the bosom of friends at the Mystic Marine Railway. We snuck under the bridge and motored around the seaport for a look before a friend drove us back to our car and trailer in Wethersfield.

The lower Connecticut would make a relaxing freshwater change of pace for an ocean sailor. It offers few challenges, only experiences. Long Island Sound was disappointing after our memories of Buzzards Bay, but with so little time spent on it, I think we'd better reserve judgment.

THE UPPER CONNECTICUT

For our upper river exploration, we chose a 40-mile stretch south of the rapids in Hartland, Vermont. My daughter, Julie, was anxious to go on this leg, so we made it a twosome. Prime canoe country, the northern river is empty of sailboats. After searching for a ramp adequate for even a Potter, we finally had to settle for a low stretch of riverbank with only a six-inch drop to the water. We backed carefully to the edge, tilted up the head of the trailer, and dropped in *Fearless*. Here the current was swifter, and we tied to a tree while I raised the mast and bent on the sails. We hung a big inner tube on a line behind the boat. Julie climbed in and we shoved off. Bettina waved us off and returned south with the car and trailer.

The current shot us along downstream. A snow-white egret watched us from the riverbank, then, as we approached, rose into the air and glided nonchalantly downstream. Soon we were around the next bend and bearing down on the egret again. Again he drifted off downstream. We tailed him for a good half hour until, the limits of his territory reached, he flapped back upstream over our heads. All this was a distraction for me. Julie, happily awash in her inner tube, was singing at the top of her lungs. Gradually I became aware that the current was moving more swiftly than ever. The power engineers, mindful of the dinnertime needs of central Vermonters, were releasing water over the dam upstream and taking it out over the dam at Bellows Falls below us. As we rounded the next bend, I found myself looking down the river at white water! The water shoaled rapidly to less than a foot and we started to really move. I rapidly pulled up the centerboard, the kick-up rudder and the outboard, broke out the oars, and rowed standing up, facing forward. The rocky bottom flew past and Julie tightened her grip on the line and sang louder than ever. We stayed in the channel and never touched a thing. Downriver apiece, we repeated the process again. Slowly the color returned to my knuckles. Julie finally started getting cold and I reeled her in. Moral: Late summer on the Connecticut means low water; late afternoon on the Connecticut means maximum current. We were lucky.

The wind died with the sun and we cranked up the little Elliott. The river widened, cornfields appeared, and we anchored for dinner and the night. Julie had brought along a flat package of popcorn that pops under a puff of aluminum foil, but we held it too low over the concentrated flame of the propane stove. Suddenly the container burst into flames and we tossed it in panic over the side. So much for the midnight snack. Out came the citronella candles to ward off the bugs and we sat talking in the dark. The humid shoreside choir sent up a roar of song and we sat together with our candle. Talk ran out and we just snuggled; finally we crawled into our bunks, setting the porta-potty in its nighttime spot on the cockpit floor. Stars revolved over the open hatch until we were tranced into sleep.

Generally, there are three rules about sailing on a river you can follow. The wind will, more often than not, blow in the direction opposite from the one you intend to go; the wind also will usually tend to follow the channel, even when the river bends; and finally, even when the wind roils the tops of the trees, not all that much will get down to you. The second day, we motored almost continuously. The engineers, content to let the water level rise quietly, had evidently cancelled the morning current. The motor buzzed; Julie resumed her position in the tube, and the scenery, pleasant but monotonous, crept by. By late afternoon we pulled into the launch ramp north of Bellows Falls, Vermont. We'd had a good time together but I wouldn't bother to go again. I missed the sandy beaches we had enjoyed on the lower Connecticut, and on any boat other than a Potter, we would have torn out the bottom. If you're planning to explore the Connecticut, I'd leave the upper section to the canoes.

THE MIDDLE CONNECTICUT

There is an inland section of the river you can get to easily on Interstate 91 that I'd recommend highly. Putting in at Oxbow Marina in Northampton, Massachusetts, you can motorsail north more than thirty-five miles. Swimming is good over a clean sandy bottom, and an abundance of islands and clean beaches where you can pitch a tent ashore and stay awhile. Here's a perfect way to beat a heatwave and get your children familiar with a new sailboat. No pressure, no *mal-de-mer,* no boredom, just a lot of swimming, camping, and easy river travel. Best of all, this stretch of river seems really *clean.*

Cleanliness is a hit-or-miss thing on the Connecticut. Farmers manure their fields and the run-off carries it down to the river. That's a natural and inevitable process and there's nothing anyone can do. Many towns along the river still have rather casual approaches to waste disposal. An effluent pipe here, a tannery discharge there leave a nagging element of doubt for the boatman or the swimmer, especially since new findings indicate that pollutants may be absorbed as readily through the pores of the skin as by passing through the intestinal tract.

Fall is coming now. As the foliage turns, we'll have still another enticement to ease on down the river a piece. We've found some favorite spots. The midday sun will have enough warmth still in it for a bracing swim and we'll enjoy the mild surprise as new vistas open up around each bend. We like real *sailing* too much to make a steady diet of it, but it's a nice change of pace, just for "messing around in boats." Water Rat knew about all that long ago. He was, after all, a River Rat too.

Lakes of the Atlantic Northeast

WINNIPESAUKEE

Nestled in beautiful, mountainous countryside, Lake Winnipesaukee is the largest of New Hampshire's freshwater lakes. The movie *On Golden Pond* was filmed at nearby Squam Lake. The area has much to recommend it: wilderness campgrounds, boating, amusement parks, and fine restaurants.

New Hampshire does not recognize boat registration from other states, nor does it permit mariners to anchor at will along the shorelines of its lakes. Visitors must register their boats anew in New Hampshire and must obtain written permission from landowners before anchoring off shorefronts. If you plan to stay at a waterfront campground or overnight at one of the lake's marinas, there's no problem. If budgetary restraints or a desire for privacy make you prefer to cruise on your own, New Hampshire makes it difficult. The place has been designed not only to entice the tourist to spend money but to *require* it.

LAKE CHAMPLAIN

Lake Champlain, straddling the northern New York-Vermont border, is 110 miles long, rimmed by mountains, and blessed with a variety of cruising conditions. The southern part of the lake is narrow—almost like a river. (You can pass by canal to the Hudson River.) The middle of the lake opens and offers honest big-water sailing. You can depart from either the New York or the Vermont shoreline with whatever state registration you might happen to have. You can anchor freely too; Vermont's car license plates may not read "Live Free or Die" as New Hampshire's do, but the idea is practiced here. Visit Burlington and sample Ben & Jerry's ice cream. The town has a good marina with a ramp—all within easy walking distance of shops and good places to eat.

Need a full-service marina? Nearby Shelburne Shipyard has a ramp and hoist. Several islands are an easy sail from either location. (Watch for poison ivy before you turn the kids loose to explore the islands.)

The northern portion of the lake is laced with small islands with many campgrounds; you could create a base camp and explore the region by boat from one of them. Another canal and the Richelieu River can take you to the St. Lawrence River. Remembering the southern canal connection to the Hudson, you might allow yourself to get delusions of grandeur and imagine a *long* inland voyage. If time permits, why not?

Champlain is one of our favorite places on the East Coast. The rocky shoreline and the ability of Champlain to whip up big seas in its open

You can sit at anchor and listen to a concert at Shelburne Farms on Lake Champlain. Courtesy of Vermont Travel Division.

section deserve respect. The northern section would be an ideal **novice** sailing ground. One could gain **mariner**'s experience out in the open lake too. This is a marvelous location!

BRAS D'OR LAKE

Imagine a stretch of picturesque coastline wrapped around an unspoiled pastoral setting. What you've got exists in the real world in the Canadian maritime province of Nova Scotia. You may have some driving to do—400 miles north to Cape Breton Island from Bangor, Maine—but check your road atlas and see what kind of scenery you'll be driving through. This is what you might call "protected maritime" sailing. Local people are helpful and friendly; the provincial government will send you plenty of useful information. The nearby ocean is definitely *not* **novice** class water, though. Huge tides, especially in the Bay of Fundy, plus fog and a rocky coast call for **expert** seamanship and a well-found boat. There's something here for sailors of every degree of expertise. Don't forget to sample the lobster.

OTHER LAKES OF INTEREST

If you write for literature from Maine and Quebec, you'll get numerous suggestions for sailing on Maine's Sebago Lake, Moosehead Lake, and Quebec's Lac Memphremagog, to name a few. If you're new to sailing, plan to camp a lot in tents, and to enjoy low-stress puttering around in beautiful settings. Any or several of these deserve your consideration.

Bays of the Atlantic Northeast

NARRAGANSETT BAY

If you're looking for wind and hearty sailing conditions, this is a good place. The coast is rocky, so approach with care and with charts. The fair-weather southwest wind piles good waves up the bay. You can find milder conditions sailing down the Sakonnet River on the east side of Aquidneck Island (also called Rhode Island). Points of interest include Newport, on the southwest side of Aquidneck Island, Bristol, Rhode Island, up the bay, and Jamestown Island (also called Conanicut). The bay is one of the principal yachting centers in the world, and is steeped in history—and money. Ramps in Newport are mediocre; the place is not laid out with small boats uppermost in mind. Let yourself get lost in the shuffle and you'll have fun. Restaurants are *very* good. The waters around here are congested, rocky, and breezy. **Mariner** class sailing.

BUZZARDS BAY

Much of what I've said about Narragansett Bay holds true here, especially about shoreline and sailing conditions. Like San Francisco Bay on the West Coast, Buzzards Bay is famous for its stiff breezes—the locals call it "the afternoon hurricane." There are plenty of good harbors on both sides of the bay. You can reach back and forth across the bay from harbor to harbor in big swells. It's fun. Mind the commercial traffic headed in and out of the Cape Cod Canal. Spend the night in Onset, then do the canal with a favorable tide. Any harbor that looks good on a road map will have enough room for a small boat. I think I've spent the night in all of them at least once. West Falmouth, Onset, and Mattapoisett are the friendliest, in our experience. This is a good place to gain experience in **mariner** conditions.

NANTUCKET SOUND AND CAPE COD BAY

Though most of New England's bays are rockbound, here the shores are sandy. Anchoring is easier and more secure; you can beach your boat. The south shore of Cape Cod is strewn with harbors just made for small boats. The north shore has fewer harbors; Barnstable is the best one, especially for **novice** sailors. It's big enough to happily occupy you for a day or maybe two, with sandbars that appear with low tide for beaching and swimming. Kids can snoop for hermit crabs. Sail out into pretty Cape Cod Bay for more elbowroom, on miles and miles of sandy beaches. Harbors are scarcer as you head north, but Wellfleet is a beautiful spot. Then there's Provincetown all the way out. It's a passage of some 25 miles from Provincetown across Cape Cod Bay to Plymouth Harbor, where you'll find good beaches for swimming. And it's fun to sail up to the *Mayflower* at its dock.

Boston Harbor isn't the cleanest place in the world, but it's an interesting blend of urban and rustic scenery. Launch from Hingham Bay and begin snooping around from there, following a fair southwest wind through the harbor to Lynn Harbor, just north of the city.

THE MAINE COAST

This is the fabled Down East country with fishing harbors mingling with tourist havens up and down the coast. There are zillions of little coves and islands sprinkled along the shoreline. You can spend a lifetime poking around and getting to know the place.

The same features that make Maine scenic require your caution. A rockbound coast is unforgiving of mistakes. You cannot casually beach anywhere; if rising swells pick up your boat and hammer it down on a

The southern coast of Cape Cod is dotted with pretty harbors such as Harwich Port, Mass.

rocky bottom, things will come unglued in a hurry. The water's cold here; you don't want to be doggie paddling in it a mile offshore near some submerged rocks you didn't expect to find. Then too, south or southeast winds can quickly blow in dense fog. Currents, tidal and otherwise, can then begin playing hob with your dead reckoning skills . . . well, you get the idea. If you're new to all this, start out easy. Fortunately, you have your choice of beautiful bays in which to begin.

Saco Bay. Sail out of Saco, Biddeford, or any of several small towns around the bay. Three state parks are in the neighborhood: Ferry Beach, Scarborough Beach, and Two Lights. Saco is relatively small compared with Casco, the next bay just around the corner.

Casco Bay. The city of Portland graces the southern corner of Casco Bay. There are a number of close-in islands to explore. These make this a good place to begin exploring Maine.

Linekin and Muscongus Bays. There are some deep indentations in the coastline here to provide sheltered sailing, including the Kennebec River. Popham Beach State Park is here, along with some colorful shoreside towns: Boothbay Harbor, Damariscotta, Wiscassett, and New Harbor, to name a few. There are some scenic islands well offshore, but I'd recommend them to an **expert** sailor only. This area alone can be a small-boater's vacation.

Penobscot Bay. Along with Frenchman Bay farther Down East, Penobscot Bay is the largest and most intricate cruising ground on the Maine coast. Islands and coves abound. You can hobnob with fancy yachts one day, with lobstermen the next, and find yourself in a corner all your own the third. Camden, Rockport, Belfast, and Bar Harbor are all within a sailor's reach. In the area are four state parks and the magnificent Acadia National Park on Mount Desert Island and parts of Isle au Haut, the Cranberry Islands, and the Schoodic Peninsula.

Charts and tide tables are a must, as are screens for your hatches. Black flies and other bloodsuckers can be a problem around here. The outer islands are interesting destinations for expert sailors in well-equipped boats. (Visit Vinalhaven on Vinalhaven Island.) Sample the lobster anywhere; if you happen to meet any lobstermen on their boats, ask if they have any softshell lobster to sell.

There are some 3,000 islands off the Maine coast. A small-boat "trail" has been established along the offshore islands leading to Acadia National Park and beyond. Campsites are available. This area can be breathtakingly beautiful, but the waters here should be treated with respect. I would not recommend the trail for **novice** sailors, but it would be a memorable treat for **mariners** or **expert** small-boat sailors. Sailors new to saltwater sailing would do well to start off in the region's many bays. There are so many to choose from. For more information, write the Maine Island Trail Association, 60 Ocean Street, Rockland, Maine 04841.

Sailing the Atlantic Northeast Coast

"Bays of the Atlantic Northeast" will give you a pretty good idea of what you'll find here. The Rhode Island coastline is mostly rockbound with a few sandy beaches facing the ocean. You can pull up a small boat safely on an ocean beach in very calm weather, but freshening wind can build surf and force you to launch through seas that can swamp the boat or throw it back onto its rudder for serious damage. This area is better known for its fine deepwater sailing.

Block Island is an interesting destination for an offshore passage in a small boat. Good jump-off places might be Mystic, Connecticut, or Point Judith, Rhode Island. The island is about 9 miles off Point Judith. Be sure to have charts. A sandbar off the harbor entrance must be avoided at all costs.

The Cape Cod area is sandier and more forgiving of piloting mistakes. You can visit Cuttyhunk, the outermost of the Elizabeth Islands. There's a good harbor there, provisions, a good place to eat, and semi-tame deer that show up in your path. The passages between islands (called "holes" locally) can have very swift currents and are best approached at slack tide—or avoided completely. Woods Hole is the most recommended passage, and the harbor and restaurants there are worth a stop too.

You've got two attractive islands offshore to visit too. Martha's Vineyard is quite close to the mainland and makes a good experience for a **novice** sailor. Vineyard Haven is touristy but fun. Get a marine chart and check out all the little bays you can sneak into in a shallow-draft boat. Nantucket is less than a 10-mile hop from the Vineyard. Here, you must bear in mind that Nantucket Shoals can develop a nasty chop in high winds and that for an ill-equipped boat, gear failure sends you out to sea on a prevailing westerly wind. I'm not suggesting Nantucket is an unreasonable passage for a small boat, only that it shouldn't be treated as a *casual* passage.

The inlets on Cape Cod along the Chatham bar can be rough. The northern arm of the Cape has fewer refuges until you get to Provincetown.

From Provincetown north, the Gulf Stream has departed for Europe and the water is much colder. The shoreline is rocky, and the scenery more rugged; fogs develop more easily; tides become more pronounced. In general, I'd say that coastal sailing in a small boat as you head Down East requires solid experience and a stout craft.

COASTING THE CANADIAN MARITIMES

The Bay of Fundy Region. I would not recommend sailing along the coast into this region in a small boat. A provincial government publication puts it succinctly: "This area is noted for its tremendous Fundy tides, which are the highest in the world, and the area's unsurpassable scenery. . . . It should be noted that boating on the Bay of Fundy, especially between St. Andrews and St. John, offers a challenge for even the most experienced small craft operator. Even on a calm day, there are very active tide rips, short breaking waves, and vigorous swirling currents to contend with." This is not the ideal environment for trailerable boats navigated by sailors used to more manageable waters.

The Northern Atlantic Coast. The Atlantic coast of Nova Scotia is warmed by the Gulf Stream, which thoughtfully returns to brush the area with warm, swimmable water and a more balmy climate than one might expect this far north. I'd recommend driving this most spectacular coast, and stopping and putting in wherever the local charm gets the better of you. You can snoop around the shoreline and, with local charts and advice, hop from cove to cove. It's a good way to sample a coastal garden of earthly delights when an extended coastal voyage seems imprudent.

You can take a ferry to Prince Edward Island, and easily do the same thing. The lush countryside and ocean scenery make it worth the extra trouble getting there.

Nova Scotia, a rare beauty in the Canadian Maritimes. Beneath the placid looking waters, though, the current rips. Note the difference between high and low tide in the Bay of Fundy's Minas Basin. Courtesy Nova Scotia Department of Tourism and Culture.

Getting Information: Atlantic Northeast

Connecticut Dept. of Economic Development
865 Brook Street
Rocky Hill, CT 06067
203-258-4200

Maine Publicity Bureau
97 Winthrop Street
Hallowell, ME 04347
207-289-5710

Massachusetts Office of Travel and Tourism
100 Cambridge Street, 13th Floor
Boston, MA 02202
617-727-3201

New Hampshire Office of Vacation/Travel
Box 856
Concord, NH 03301
603-271-2343

Rhode Island Dept. of Economic Development
Tourism Division
7 Jackson Walkway
Providence, RI 02903
401-277-2601

Vermont Agency of Development and Community Affairs
Travel Division
134 State Street
Montpelier, VT 05602
802-828-3236

Newfoundland Department of Tourism
PO Box 8700
St. John's
Newfoundland A1B 4J6 CANADA
709-576-2830

Tourism New Brunswick
PO Box 12345
Fredericton
New Brunswick E3B 5C3 CANADA
1-800-561-0123

Prince Edward Island Department of Tourism and Parks
Visitors Services
PO Box 940
Charlottetown
P.E.I. C1A 7M5 CANADA
902-368-4444

Quebec Office of Tourism
60 D'Auteuil Street
Quebec City
Province of Quebec G1R 4C4
 CANADA
418-692-2471

Nova Scotia Department of Tourism and Culture
Tourist Information
PO Box 456
Halifax
Nova Scotia B3J 2R5 CANADA
902-424-5005

CHAPTER 8

The Middle Atlantic States

St. Lawrence River

1

2

Lake Ontario

3

4

Niagara Falls   5   Syracuse

Buffalo

Lake Erie

NEW YORK

Hudson River

Long Island
Sound

New York
City

Long Island

PENNSYLVANIA

Philadelphia   NEW JERSEY

6

MARYLAND

Atlantic Ocean

Baltimore

13

8   7

Washington D.C.

10

12

DELAWARE

9

11   14

Approximate Miles

0   100   200

Points of Interest

1. Thousand Islands
2. Lake Champlain
3. Lake George
4. Oneida Lake
5. Finger Lakes
6. Barnegat Bay
7. Cape May
8. Delaware Bay
9. Rehoboth Bay
10. Oxford
11. Chesapeake Bay
12. Potomac River
13. Annapolis
14. Assateague Island

HERE ARE WATERWAYS closest to some of the nation's most urbanized areas. If the scenery is often less dramatic and unspoiled, there are other compensations, such as some spectacular urban waterfronts—scenery of another kind. Plus, there is more unspoiled water around than you might think.

Rivers of the Middle Atlantic

With special caution for currents and traffic, these rivers can be managed by a novice sailor.

THE HUDSON RIVER

Although the Hudson extends far north, try launching south of Albany and letting the current sweep you downstream past some spectacular countryside. The Hudson has been called America's Rhine because of its shoreside cliffs in New Jersey and because of some of the beautiful views opening as you go downriver. Although the megalopolis extends north and south of New York City, it doesn't run far upriver; you'll have miles and miles of rustic scenery. You'll have to decide whether to dock upstream of the Big Apple, retrieve your car and pull out, or to continue south until you round the last bend and the Land of Oz suddenly appears in the distance. There are all the attractions of the New York skyline and the Statue of Liberty to think of. But then there are also swift currents, sometimes dangerous floating debris to damage outboard motors, and *very* heavy and impatient commercial traffic. A commercial boat, confronted with the unhappy choice of running down a yacht or colliding with a super tanker, will hold its course and trample you under. It has no choice, when you think of it. A small sailboat hasn't the hull speed to dart quickly out of harm's way. If you choose to negotiate New York Harbor, I would suggest contacting the harbor patrol first and getting a suggested course and advance warning about conditions you might not be able to foresee. Monitor your VHF *continuously*. The working channel is 13 on your marine radio. Just in case, it's good to know Manhattan has a marina at the foot of 79th Street. You could pull out at Staten Island's Great Kills Harbor or round Brooklyn and enter Rockaway inlet into Jamaica Bay's Gateway Recreational Area. (The area occupies both sides of the river mouth.) The Hudson is one of the major commercial and historical waterways of the North American continent. Wouldn't it make an interesting project, if you find you like river sailing, to use consecutive summers to explore *all* the continent's major rivers?

THE DELAWARE RIVER

Here's another waterway steeped in colonial history. The upper Delaware runs through some lovely, pastoral countryside. You can put in as far north as Dingman's Ferry in the Delaware Water Gap Recreational area, which has a marina. Winds are apt to be light, but the current will waft you downstream. It's best to plan for a downriver end point and to take a bus back to fetch your car and trailer.

With New Jersey on one side and Pennsylvania on the other, you can sail past Washington's Crossing and Trenton to Philadelphia. From the water, Philadelphia is a spectacular display of commercial and industrial might without the shipping congestion of New York. You should, nonetheless, have more than the minimal outboard power to buck the current and get out of harm's way.

Visit Philadelphia's waterfront and tour the marine museum and Independence Plaza while you're in the area. Many of the city's cultural points of interest are within walking distance of the river. Continue downriver and end your trip at the boatyard in Essington, Pennsylvania, or enter Delaware Bay for more distant destinations on the Jersey or the Delaware shores.

THE POTOMAC RIVER

The lower part of the Potomac River is a roomy historical waterway. Put in near Washington's birthplace at Mount Vernon, Virginia and work your way north for a short sail to the nation's capital, counting on your outboard to get you the final stretch if the wind proves no help.

The Hudson, the Delaware, and the Potomac offer the chance to see some spectacular urban scenery, but don't expect pure water. The Hudson, at least at New York City, is foul, though cleanup efforts upstream (pioneered for years by Pete Seeger and his yacht *Clearwater*) have begun to pay off. When I sailed the Delaware near Philly as a boy on our family boat, I could see raw sewage floating on the surface of the water. Improvements have come, but I would restrain myself from swimming until well into tidal water—or upstream of Trenton. Likewise with the Potomac, I'd feel better swimming in tidal water, well down from the nation's capital.

Lakes of the Middle Atlantic

Although all the states in this region have small recreational lakes, New York holds all the cards when it comes to big lake sailing. Let's take a look.

THE FINGER LAKES

The last Ice Age gouged out thousands of lakes across the width of Canada and the northern U.S. Many of these, such as New York's Finger Lakes, have their long axes running north-south. The Finger Lake system runs roughly between Rochester and Syracuse, with Oneida Lake, directly northeast of Syracuse, adding to the attraction. Seneca and Cayuga, the two longest Finger Lakes, run more than 30 miles from end to end with maximum width of 4 to 5 miles. These lakes are purely recreational; there is no commercial traffic other than an occasional tour boat. The region jealously guards the water purity around here. Boatyards and ramps abound; sailing is good. **Novice** class sailors can get solid experience out there on windy days without undue risk to family or the boat itself.

ADIRONDACK PARK LAKES

The Adirondack Park is one of the treasures of the East Coast. A glance at a road map will show you a huge area in green with an area almost the size of Lake Ontario—all devoted to wilderness recreation. Lakes of all sizes abound in the confines of the park. Many of the smaller ones are rimmed mostly with private lands. Houses blend nicely into the wooded shoreline, but you can't be casual about beaching and wandering. Still, there's much to recommend the area in the way of camping as well as sailing. Write for a New York campground directory; where campgrounds border lakes, you've got the best of both worlds.

The crown jewel of the region is Lake George, nestled in the midst of the Adirondack Mountains. It's easily big enough to absorb a small boat for a week's vacation (or two) and especially palatable, all the islands on the lake are state owned. That means that you can camp on them, explore them, even tie up to state docks on them. It's all on a first-come, first-served basis. Expect weekends to be crowded; if you can begin and end your trip on a weekday, you'll avoid the crunch. Launch ramp fees are apt to be stiffer around Lake George than at most places for some reason, but it's worth it, especially if you stay for more than a day or two.

There are a multitude of other beautiful lakes here, Great Sacandaga Lake and Cranberry Lake, to name two. The park's eastern edge flanks part of Lake Champlain too. The water is clean and good for swimming everywhere.

Bays and Sounds of the Middle Atlantic

LONG ISLAND SOUND

Old-timers insist that breezes were stronger in Long Island Sound when the region was more rural. Winds on the sound seem lighter than they are farther north; a genoa is a useful sail to have aboard if you plan to sail in the sound regularly.

The Connecticut coast and the northern shore of Long Island are generously supplied with harbors, making the sound a good spot for **novice** sailors. Farther north, tidal currents flow over a shallow and narrow stretch, causing what is called a "rip"—something to be taken seriously. The northern part might be better considered **mariner**'s territory. Both shorelines are very pretty in a salty kind of way. Thunderstorms can be violent on the sound. One astonished sailor told of being hit in the face by a newspaper blown over the water all the way from New

Dabs of green freckle the St. Lawrence River in Upstate New York's appropriately named Thousand Islands region, a gunkholer's paradise. Courtesy of New York State Department of Economic Development.

York City (or Brooklyn)! Seek shelter if storms are making up. The bottom is usually muddy enough to provide good holding for your anchor.

Special points of interest: Mystic (the old whaling port and museum, Stonington, Essex, and New London, on the Connecticut shoreline, and Oyster Bay, Huntington Bay, and Orient Point on the Long Island shoreline. Gaining access to the sound via the East River is tricky as currents are very swift, especially in Hell Gate, and traffic is heavy.

DELAWARE BAY

Partially because of the water quality, and partially because its open southern end leaves Delaware Bay exposed to a southwest wind, this is the least popular of the region's large bays. The chop can be nasty here, but several interesting itineraries call for passing down or across the bay, so secure the hatches if it's rough and grin and bear it.

You'll notice the relative lack of civilization along the marshy north shore until you reach Port Norris, New Jersey. At Cape May, New Jersey, you can round up into some protected water. Along the southern shore, is a canal south of Delaware City to the Chesapeake or, farther south, another shorter canal to Rehoboth Bay at Lewes.

George Washington ordered this lighthouse on the tip of Long Island at Montauk Point built in 1795 to protect his infant country's burgeoning transatlantic trade routes. Courtesy of New York State Department of Economic Development.

CHESAPEAKE BAY

This is the largest of the Middle Atlantic bays. Like the glacial lakes, it too is a product of the last Ice Age. As the great ice sheets melted away to the north, tremendous quantities of water were released to find a path to the sea. The present Susquehanna River was then a thundering river of mythic proportions. The river carved out an enormous flood plain that is now, with volume drastically reduced and sea levels much higher, the Chesapeake Bay. The bay is approximately 180 miles long with harbors and scenic refuges lining its eastern and western shores. The water is brackish—a mixture of fresh and salt—with the salinity increasing as you head south toward the mouth of the bay. It's a boater's paradise.

On the bay's western shore sits the port of Baltimore, with an attractive yacht basin smack in the heart of the city's waterfront. (The Inland *Waterway Guide* has helpful suggestions on how to make a safe passage through the commercial traffic; see "Useful Books and Videos" in the Appendices.) Twenty miles south you'll sail into Annapolis, one of the world's principal yachting centers. Like Newport, Rhode Island, Annapolis is a colonial town with old-time charms and an overwhelmingly nautical feel. Marinas and maritime facilities abound. This may not be your least expensive stopover, however.

Farther on southwest are the Potomac River, which winds its way past Washington, D.C. to Mount Vernon, Virginia, Washington's birthplace. Farther south still, near Newport News, Virginia is Colonial National Historical Park with Williamsburg, Yorktown, and Jamestown. You can do a historical passage.

The Eastern Shore of Maryland is more laid-back but no less historical. Sail up the Choptank River to Cambridge and Oxford. You'll find the best peach ice cream in the world, and walk down quiet, shaded streets to get it. By all means go for a crab feast. They'll spread down newspapers all over your table, then deposit a heap of steaming red crabs; it's a free-for all. Leave your table manners at the door and just dig in. The crabs are spicy, the palate is traditionally cooled with beer. Or try softshell crabs.

Barrier islands, such as Assateague in Maryland, provide protected sailing areas from Maryland through Delaware, New Jersey, and New York's Long Island. Sail in bays or negotiate inlets for ocean sailing. Seashore areas offer superb beach swimming and surfcasting. The ponies are wild, descendants of the survivors of a Spanish shipwreck centuries ago. Courtesy of Maryland Tourism.

This is oyster country too. If it's Maine for lobster, it's Maryland for crabs and oysters.

There's another form of marine life in the Chesapeake that's less fun: sea nettles, a type of stinging jellyfish that proliferates as the bay warms up. They drag stinging tentacles behind their cup-shaped bodies, and when they're around swimming is risky and sailors are reduced to dumping buckets of water onto their heads to cool off. Check with the locals.

The southeastern shoreline is less populated; you can get away from it all, or visit some of the bay's islands for a step back to an even more rustic way of life.

Winds are often mild, especially in mid- to late summer, making this a good place to gather sailing skills. The shoreline is sand or mud—so learning to sail in a shoal-draft boat is like sailing in a rubber room. Thundersqualls can be violent; I've been in 110 m.p.h. winds out there on one memorable occasion. Being shallow, the bay can be very rough in high winds. Mind the weather forecasts.

ABOUT THE BARRIER ISLAND BAYS

Wave action has piled sand into islands that run along much of the Gulf and Atlantic shorelines. Behind these barrier islands, you'll often find good sailing and pleasant, sandy scenery. Access to the ocean is available through inlets, but these inlets can be treacherous. Often they're shoal, tempting seas to break at the inlet's mouth. The currents and waves shift around the sand, making charts obsolete. And finally when wind and tide run in opposite directions—or in heavy seas—inlets can be *very* dangerous. Slack tide and fine weather—teamed with and up-to-date charts, are the best combination. Some local advice doesn't hurt either.

Long Island's Bays. Long Island offers miles and miles of protected sailing. Middle Bay, East Bay, Great South Bay, and Oyster Bay are just a few. Expect a lot of powerboat traffic. This area serves an enormous urban population and facilities are plentiful. The northeastern extremity of the island offers a more rural feel and more elbow room. If you're approaching from New England, a ferry from New London, Connecticut can haul your car and boat to Orient Point, saving you 150 miles of heavily congested travel.

Barnegat Bay. Most of New Jersey's oceanfront shoreline is fringed with barrier islands, forming sandy-bottomed Barnegat Bay. The Inland *Waterway Guide* offers advice on the bay's inlets. Shallow-draft sailboats can have a lot of fun in the Barnegat. The clear water (where powerboats haven't churned it up) makes for agreeable skin-diving. You'll find wilderness isolation and frenetic shoreside activity; the kids may enjoy the boardwalk entertainments. So might you, if you pull into Atlantic City and have some decent clothes. There are no sea nettles here and the usually benign weather makes this a **novice** sailor's paradise.

The Delmarva Barrier Bays. South of Delaware Bay, the ocean has formed a series of islands that contain Rehoboth Bay, and a string of bays inside Assawoman, Assateague, and Chincoteague Islands. Assateague Island is a National Seashore—protected from development, and an ideal vacation location. These areas are worth a look—and it's a pleasant drive through Maryland cornfields to the Chesapeake's Eastern Shore.

Sailing the Middle Atlantic Coast

Basically, a coastal passage along the Middle Atlantic States is a hop from barrier island to barrier island from Virginia all the way to Fishers Island at the northern extremity of Long Island. Unless you're contemplating an extended coastal passage in a small boat, I'd be tempted to ask, "Why bother?" The bay sailing opportunities are so wonderful. If you do come around outside the Delmarva Peninsula (so named because it includes parts of Delaware, Maryland, and Virginia), there is a maze of small islands north of the Chesapeake Bay Bridge/Tunnel. The areas behind these can be shoal and a bit buggy. You could do the barrier bays with

---

Sailing America: Peachblossom Creek

Once in a while, we get to travel across not only a map, but through time. Crabbing is neither an idea for me nor a hobby; it's a memory. We drove across the Peachblossom Creek on our way down to Oxford. There on the far bank was the old boathouse with its sweeping pagoda roof and, in the big house, were cousins and people long loved and seldom seen since my childhood. I wandered down the bank to the boathouse. One door sticks now. Rather than break it, I used another. Floats, old coils of rotting line hung with the cobwebs and the waspnests—old gray bonecolored ones and fresh new ones, light tan. There were always wasps hanging in the air and glittering when they lit like samurai warriors. The place still had its smell.

Of all our senses, maybe smell is the one most closely connected to memory. (If that's true, maybe animals remember far more vividly than we can imagine.) But there I was, almost in tears over a subtle mixture of mildew, shellfish, old wood, hemp, cedar and salt. How can I explain to my children without boring them to death? How can we point to a blank wall and say, "there it is, don't you see?" To our children, the past is a phantom; the world a delicate, fragile place.

In Oxford, old Wiley's boatyard still stands—now called Cutts & Case. Ralph Wiley died some years ago, but his wife still lives there. Plink, the foreman, still lives there. Same broad face and peaked cap. Boats still pull out on a massive rusted chain. Piles of boatyard trash in the same places, crunch of oyster shells underfoot. The battered metal coke machine is in the same corner. It still works. What do I feel? Gratitude, that's what. I'm grateful that my cousins have kept up the boathouse. I'm glad the piano is in the same spot in the huge living room, that Plink is still alive.

There are only a few people on earth who can walk around Wiley's boatyard and feel anything like I do. That's what family is, maybe. Forget genetics. Family is people who have been significant companions on our inner journeys. If you don't have to explain it to people, they're family. Suddenly I feel very sorry for only children.

I had a Coke from the old machine. Little glass bottle used over and over. Maybe it was just my imagination, but I don't remember tasting one so good in years.

occasional outside passages to get from one bay to the next, but that would have you running a lot of inlets—an interesting challenge for an **expert** sailor. It would take time. Reliable charts, a tide timetable, and good advice all would help.

Getting Information: Middle Atlantic

New York Department of Economic Development
Tourism Division
99 Washington Avenue
Albany, NY 12245
518-474-4116

New Jersey Department of Tourism
20 West State Street
Trenton, NJ 08625-0826
609-292-2470

Pennsylania
1-800-VISIT-PA
(800-847-4872)

Delaware Office of Tourism and Development
99 King's Highway, Room 1401
Dover, DE 19903
302-736-4271

Maryland Office of Tourism Development
217 East Redwood Street
Baltimore, MD 21202
301-333-6611

CHAPTER 9

The Atlantic Southeast

Points of Interest
1. Chesapeake Bay
2. Albemarle Sound
3. Pamlico Sound
4. Neuse River
5. Onslow Bay
6. Winyah Bay
7. Charleston Harbor
8. St. Helena Sound
9. Port Royal Sound/Hilton Head
10. Ft. Frederica
11. Cumberland Island
12. Jacksonville/St. Johns River
13. Indian River Lagoon/
    Canaveral National Seashore
14. Biscayne Bay
15. Florida Bay
16. Lake Okeechobee

THE ATLANTIC Southeast has its main assets tied up in its coastal waterways. The rivers and lakes of this region are not the drawing cards that will cause someone to haul a small boat half a continent, but the shoreline attractions might do it. Let's take a look.

The Intracoastal Waterway

The Intracoastal Waterway system doesn't fit neatly into the regional system with which we're classifying things in this book because it unites coastal regions and waterways into a network through which a mariner can pass from the Annisquam River in Massachusetts all the way down the Atlantic coast to Florida and around the Gulf of Mexico to Brownsville, Texas. There is a need for an occasional short outside passage, but canals stitch the various bays together into an integrated system. Small boats share the waterway with barges and other commercial traffic. The *Waterway Guides* give useful information for the whole route and, in the process, for anyone wanting to sail in any body of water covered by the waterway system. Most vacationers won't have the time to traverse the waterway for any great distance, but we'll discuss it piecemeal as we lay out the points of interest in each region of the Atlantic and Gulf Coast.

Lakes of the Atlantic Southeast

LAKE OKEECHOBEE

By far the largest lake in this region is Lake Okeechobee in southern Florida. A series of canals connects this huge lake with the Atlantic coast some 30 miles away. Another canal runs from Moore Haven on the lake's western shore to the Caloosahatchee River on the Gulf Coast, so it's possible to sail or motor all the way across Florida rather than transit the rest of the coastline—100 miles as opposed to 240 miles. For someone headed through the waterway for points west, this is an important savings. The lake is a destination in its own right for anyone interested in fishing, sailing, and sampling the wildlife of the deep south. Southerners, more adapted to hot climes than Yankees like me, will likely take its summer temperatures with more grace. Good mosquito netting is vital here. Beware of thunderstorms; Florida has more of them than any state in the Union. If you're well secured, they can actually become one of the state's attractions, providing awesome displays of Nature's power and temporarily cooling things off in the process.

INLAND LAKES

Near Chattanooga, the Tennessee River is dammed up to produce Chickamauga Lake. Like most of the lakes produced in this way, it's fairly narrow (a mile or so) but quite long, with many byways to explore. There are a number of lakes formed in this manner in the region. The Savannah River on the Georgia-South Carolina border produces two unusually lengthy lakes: Clark Hill and Hartwell lakes. More dams produce two smaller lakes farther north on the Savannah. The Savannah River itself offers this region's best chance for a scenic river trip ending at Georgia's beautiful

Guitarist Sam Dorsey passed me in his Marshall catboat heading south to Florida—into the heat.

port city, Savannah. At that point, a sailor could join the Intracoastal Waterway. All of the lakes mentioned would be ideal locations for **novice** sailors.

Bays of the Atlantic Southeast

North Carolina is home to a number of barrier island bays and sounds, some big, some not. All are shallow and can be subject to nasty sea conditions when the wind gets up—especially when strong winds oppose tides. Weather forecasts should be noted several times a day. These bays provide good sailing for a **mariner** and would provide a challenge for a **novice,** provided he has a motor along to get out of trouble should the need arise. You can enter Currituck Sound on the C&A Canal from Norfolk, Virginia. Or you can take a decidedly more rustic trek on the Dismal Swamp Canal to Albemarle Sound. In both cases, you'll need a dependable motor and a enough gas to carry you some 20 miles if you choose the C&A, or some 40 miles if you choose the Great Dismal.

The Intracoastal Waterway takes you through the 22-mile Alligator-Pungo Canal, bypassing a large piece of Pamlico Sound, the largest barrier island bay. Should you choose to go the less-traveled eastern route, you can visit Kitty Hawk and Nag's Head, continuing along the Cape Hatteras and Cape Lookout National Seashores. Here you can camp on sandy beaches and hike over dunes to the ocean beaches—or you can sail along for mile after uninhabited mile of boggy coastline, reprovisioning at Engelhard or Swanquarter, N.C. The only indication that these rural locations exist will be a line of alternately red and green markers that you follow into shore. Should you want to put in along this route, there's a ramp at Big Trout Marina in Engelhard, owned by gracious folks.

In the middle of Pamlico Sound, you may spot a stationary Navy warship on the horizon. Lest you be tempted to sail on over for a look, be warned that it's a *gunnery target* for Navy planes; stay well clear at all times. The mouth of the Neuse River is a sailing ground all in itself. There's a ramp in New Bern, should you want to start a trip there. The waterway runs from the Neuse south to Morehead City, through a short canal. A small boat can sail through Core Sound along the National Seashore and avoid some of the big-boat traffic. Eventually, you'll wind up in skinny Bogue Sound, the last of North Carolina's major barrier bays.

The barrier islands continue almost without interruption to Cape Fear and the South Carolina border. The waters around Charleston, South Carolina, the sounds on either side of Beaufort (Saint Helena and Port Royal), and the port of Savannah, Georgia are all scenic sailing grounds. Choose one, or hit them all in a series, but do so by car; the trip is far less tedious than by sea.

For the most part, the Intracoastal Waterway proceeds south to the tip of Florida with no major bays along the route. Where the Waterway turns inland, it can be buggy and breathless in midsummer. We'll pass over areas of interest to the deepwater cruiser in favor of places you can drive to and launch your boat.

THE BANANA AND INDIAN RIVER LAGOONS (CAPE CANAVERAL SEASHORE AREA)

Here are waterways with lots to recommend them. Shoal-draft boats can find actual privacy, skimming over sand flats to unoccupied beaches. The John F. Kennedy Space Center lies along your route and if you time your visit to a launch, it can make for a spectacular day. The Vertical Assembly Building, where the moon rockets were put together, is so huge that its bulk will stay on your horizon hour after hour. This is a winter destination with real potential.

BISCAYNE BAY

This area can be really hot in summer, but suppose you wanted to get away in the winter and bring your boat? Sailing here is great; you're near the port of Miami and there's a wonderful marina right inside Government Cut. Sample barrier island beaches and never be as far away from civilization as it seems. This, as are the smaller sounds, is a marvelous place for **novice** sailors.

FLORIDA BAY

When I first saw this place on a map, I assumed that all these islands were composed of white sand, each with at least a palm tree or two. In fact, much of Florida Bay has a muddy bottom. Don't let that discourage you, though. Florida Bay offers a chance to navigate quite a distance without ever being out of sight of some sort of land. This is a shoal-draft sailboat heaven. Be sure you've got effective bug screens for dawn and dusk attacks—or just jump in and stay in until dark. If you're sailing this area in summer, rigging some kind of sunshade will give you needed protection. You can buy cheap umbrellas with clamps on the bottom, meant for beach chairs. If the winds aren't too strong, clamp them onto cockpit rails

Shoal-draft boats make beaching and exploring the Florida Keys a delight. We're at Bahia Honda Key.

to give you some shade. Summer winds are usually light; a genoa would be a good sail down here. Watch out for thunderstorms throughout the region. Winds can be violent in storms and they can move into your path with astonishing speed.

Sailing the Atlantic Southeast Coast

Some of the best sailing in this region is along the Florida Keys, where you can dodge behind the shelter of a friendly island if foul weather threatens. The Gulf Stream passes within a few miles of the Florida coast. Occasionally you can see its darker blue hue from shore. While the stream can boost your northward passage by some 4 to 5 knots, violent sea conditions develop rapidly when northerly winds oppose the flow of the current, especially in shallower water. Oceangoing yachts have been beaten to pieces in Gulf Stream storms. At such times, the stream is no place for a small boat.

At the Georgia border, the Cumberland and St. Simons Islands make for good cruising, as do the island-dotted shorelines of South Carolina and the southern end of the Delmarva Peninsula. You can run in and out of little islands all day, swimming as you like, beaching, and sampling scenery.

Do not attempt to sail outside of Cape Hatteras. This area is a graveyard of huge ships. When winds and currents oppose each other in the relatively shoal waters off the cape, terrifying sea conditions develop. Even if you consider yourself an **expert,** why risk it when the Pamlico passage is prettier and safer? Long passages have been accomplished in small boats, but if our discussion here involves places we can trailer to—especially with our families, you can get all the excitement you want inside the barrier islands. I sampled a howling black squall complete with hail and enough lightning to power a small city for an hour *inside* Cape Hatteras. I shudder to think what it was like outside.

Sailing America: Frying on the ICW

"An adventure is an inconvenience rightly considered."
E. K. Chesterton

It was an idea I had been savoring for a long time: to get away from it all for a few weeks and just let the summer wind blow me up the Atlantic coast. It made sense to do this in a place I had never been, to cover new ground. I'd never sailed in the South. Why not start in Florida and explore the Intracoastal Waterway?

This also seemed the occasion for a new boat—something with room to actually *live* on. After years of cruising on *Fearless,* my Potter 15, I got a Potter 19, with three times the interior volume, beds for everyone in the family, and still a small boat. Here was the plan: as soon as school ended (for me as well as my daughters), we'd trailer our new boat *Tanbark* down to the Miami Beach Marina. Bettina, my wife, would fly down to join us. We'd sail around Biscayne

Bay for a few days, then the girls would drive north on a leisurely route, towing the trailer home.

During the winter, the snow fell outside the window while I pored over charts and *Waterway Guides,* planning the route. Spring was occupied moving aboard *Tanbark,* equipping her for extended cruising. This is a delicious phase, relishing a trip in advance, carrying your ideas around inside yourself like a child. Then it was June and we were off down I-95. From Virginia on, I watched the scenery fly by and imagined myself crawling like a bug back up the southern face of America. It was starting to get hot.

The Miami Beach Marina was friendly and attractive. Bettina flew in and we spent the night panting and perspiring in our bunks.

"Record heat," they said.

Interest in a family cruise evaporated.

"Sure you don't want to come back to Cape Cod with us?" Tina asked.

No. I was committed and after a day or two on the beach and a night or two in cool hotels, we went our separate ways; the gang disappeared up the causeway to the mainland; I cast off and headed out Government Cut to the Atlantic. Almost immediately, the wind rounded to the northeast and thunderstorms marched down on little *Tanbark.* The next several hours yielded intervals of progress punctured by powerful gusts slamming into the rigging, rain, and lightning. And the east wind was getting up a nasty surf; this would never do.

Baker's Haulover Inlet appeared and it seemed prudent to get out of a deteriorating situation. Heading toward shore, the water turned emerald and translucent. A sea turtle appeared in my wake, looking confused, then dolphins showed up. I wondered if Wagner on the stereo might attract their interest, so I turned the volume up, to no avail. Wind and tide were in opposition at Baker's Haulover, so as the seas began approaching the vertical, I banged my way in with the Eska at full howl and Wagner at full crescendo. At this point I learned not to look back over my shoulder when running inlets. A motorboat with far more horsepower than *Tanbark* hit a wave and hurtled straight into the air. Then things suddenly eased; I was inside, ready to sample the delights of the Intracoastal Waterway for the first time.

At first, *Tanbark* soared ahead, but the wind grew light and fluky, settling at last in a contrary direction. More thunderstorms rolled by, then the air quieted and the heat soared. It was a long motor through a thousand backyards, and a reminder of the affluence of America. Mile after mile the new houses rolled by, yachts parked on the waterway. Few people though, almost no children. Here was the massed stuff of the American Dream preserved in the suffocating heat as if under an evacuated bell jar. A palace floated by looking like a garish mausoleum, with pillars and statuary arrayed in pastel symmetry.

The heat was relentless. I imagined the Eska felt it too, I throttled it back to a mutter and sat in a daze as the hours rolled by. I ended up pulling into Fort Lauderdale in the dark. Snooping down a canal, I found a section of dock and a hose under which I sat for about twenty minutes, enjoying the cool relief. Thunderstorms swept the boat several times, rousting me out to close the hatches and stifle until they passed. This was Day 1; I had covered 20 miles. Only 980 miles, give or take, to go.

A static high pressure system blanketed the East Coast, from Florida almost to Maine. It was to become the dominant reality of my cruise: Each day the sun came up smoking red. Each morning I imagined I was being ironed flat under the Florida sun; around noon thunderheads would begin to boil up along the inland horizon like thermonuclear explosions, the afternoon wind machine. Sometimes the afternoon thermals pulled in a useful beam wind; often, as on rivers, the wind would settle into an up-channel or down-channel course. By late afternoon, the thunderheads would have matured. Sometimes the onshore thermal drafts held them off, sometimes not, and the wind would round to the north. Under such conditions it seemed imprudent to venture back out into the ocean. The winds were too unreliable to deliver a small boat from one all-weather inlet to the next within the span of a solo sailor's endurance. Also, the daily thunderstorms, despite their familiarity, deserved respect. Their occasional violence was more safely sampled in the waterway. With a sailing partner, an offshore coasting route would have made good sense, but in conditions of unusual heat, long endurance is not a thing to be counted on. And more than anything else, I remember the continuous blur of heat, of my skin retaining the heat—and then glowing with that heat even in the dark so that when the evening wind died, I lay in my bed and felt the sun on me still.

I began to develop some countermeasures. A foot mat could be soaked with water and thrown on the cockpit sole to provide relative coolness underfoot. A surgeon's gown and a wide-brimmed hat could be wetted down. I got used to leaving a trail of puddles in my wake as I moved about the boat. With the relative humidity hovering between 85 and 90%, the cooling cycle worked between a range of soaked and damp. At damp, all benefits stopped. Everything was damp. A half cap of fabric softener takes the eventual clamminess out of saltwater solar showers, preserving the freshwater supply for drinking and a good rinse-off at day's end. Rotating hats through the ice chest provided regular treats too, though neither the hats nor the ice chest grew less fragrant. The day's final treat always consisted of a cooling rub-down with a turkish towel that had sat all day in the bottom of the fridge. I'd end by wrapping it around my head and leaning back against the aft cabin bulkhead for a few minutes.

Most important in such conditions is some kind of cockpit awning. Many of the sailboats I passed in the waterway motored the whole way rather than take down the awnings that sheltered the cockpit and often the cabins. I had rigged *Tanbark* with a makeshift Bimini that crossed the cockpit with a narrow band of shade. It was freestanding, so I could sail with it up. Storms broke it up a few times, but never beyond repair. It's a *must* in tropical waters.

Sun and heat will drain your body of fluids at a dangerous rate, even if you drink a lot. My urine output dropped below 6 ounces a day. I was often dizzy and spaced—another reason why I found myself avoiding the very ocean sailing I had looked forward to for so long. A bottle of wine cooler flattened me one night. I had saved it as a special treat; now my usual distrust of alcohol on the water has even more conviction. Extreme heat magnifies alcohol's impact many-fold, and its dangers. After trying a lot of fluids, I settled on bulk quantities of Gatorade. After a week, I located some salt tablets—buffered to reduce the likelihood of stomach cramps. My rate of perspiration slowed and the dizziness eased.

I found also that my posterior was beginning to rebel at sitting damp for so long on non-absorbant substances. Talcum powder helped at night but by day, my backside hide yearned for fresh air. Once in desperation, I powdered and diapered myself with a beach towel. The solution came in the form of a wire mesh seat cover from an automotive supply shop. What they lack in softness, they make up for in ventilation.

North of Florida's St. Lucie Inlet, soaring along with a beam wind for 50 miles, I got a taste of what *Tanbark* could do with a day of useful wind. The waterway was opening into a beautiful stretch: the Indian River. In more temperate weather, this would be a small-boater's paradise, especially the Indian River Lagoon. A sailor with some time could sample the Banana River, Cape Canaveral, hike over sand dunes to ocean beaches, and enjoy the marvelous fishing and the flourishing wildlife. A deep-draft boat might be more limited, but most of the shoal-draft compact and micro-cruising boats could have the run of the place. *Tanbark* draws six inches with its daggerboard raised, so I could go pretty much where I pleased. At one point, I was attracted by loud squawking and drifted over to watch a pair of snowy egrets circling and strutting and fluffing their plumage—something about romance, I think.

I laid over at Marineland about 30 miles north of Daytona Beach, saw the divers do their 20,000 Leagues Under the Sea routine, though the nostalgic costumes probably meant less to the present flock of kids. I was raised on Disney, they on Jacques Cousteau. It was fun to see the dolphins strut their stuff. One can only hope their lives in captivity make up in variety and intensity the lives they lost when they lost the sea. Marineland is quite a complex, with guest slips, a launch ramp with parking, both a campground and a hotel, and a good ocean beach. It would make a good base camp for a trailer-sailing expedition.

As the waterway nears Georgia, the channel becomes more convoluted. In the heat, I found it tedious and looked forward to ducking back out into the Atlantic, where I imagined the wind would be better. The Jacksonville inlet was a refreshing change; here was a bustling seaport with all kinds of heavy commercial traffic, whirling helicopters from the Mayport naval base, and a boiling tide streaming in the channel. After a long motor, I was back in the ocean at last. Then the wind died. Here I made a mistake. It would have been prudent seamanship in a small boat to have turned about, let the current hustle me back in and boost me up the waterway toward the next inlet. Or I could have anchored inside and gotten a fresh start out the inlet the next morning. I was too impatient to leave the hot tedium of the waterway behind me, so with only a few hours of useful wind and light left in the day, out I went. The expanded horizon was a tonic for my soul; despite the light wind, I refused to motor anymore. Progress was pleasant but slow. The light was turning orange, then pink as an inlet appeared, though I knew it wasn't the one I wanted. Should I press on under a full moon and go for St. Marys? The wind was very light; it could take all night. Could I stay awake all night alone? No, I was already tired.

The sea around me was calm. How bad could the inlet be? I headed in, enjoying the sunset's palette and the rising moon. Closing in, I could see two areas with breakers with what appeared to be a channel running between them. Purely as a precautionary measure, I started my outboard. Then the wind died. It seemed odd that I should be closing with the shoreline as rapidly as I was and I climbed onto the cabintop to furl the sail and get a better look. In the fading light, my depth perception was off and from even a slightly elevated perspective, it was clear I had gotten myself into trouble. As I jumped down into the cockpit, the open zone between the breakers dissolved. A breaker suddenly appeared and slammed broadside into *Tanbark,* sending her wallowing in its wake. I scrambled for the outboard's throttle and, looking down, saw bottom. The daggerboard grounded and a second wave landed with a bang and a shower of spray. The board was jammed in its trunk, prompting a frantic visit to the cabin. We got hit twice more before I could wrestle up the board. *Tanbark* yielded more easily to the next one then, safely behind the bar, I revved up the motor and banged my way back out through the breakers into safe waters. Another smaller set of breakers was negotiated more easily, then I was free to approach the passage, my heart pounding, my knees suddenly wobbly. A quick survey revealed no damage. No solid water had come over the rail; the cabin was totally dry—even of spray. Clearly, my Potter had taken better care of me than I had of it.

I cleared an unmanned drawbridge by hiking out from the shrouds and heeling the boat sufficiently to sneak under. By then it was dark and after 14 hours of sailing, I was baffled by the channel lights. I anchored to a breathless night of heat, bugs, and paranoia. I imagined my anchor dragging, eventually carrying me out to sea while I slept. Around the boat, the moon shone down, fish leaped and splashed, and under the hull, creatures made sounds like someone shelling nuts or cracking his knuckles.

The next morning dawned hot and windless. The water temperature was 87°. I fired up the Eska and headed north. I dragged into Fernandina Beach near the Georgia border wilted and discouraged, only to fall into the hospitality of a perfect stranger, Gary Hill, the local Potter dealer. Did I need a shower? Dinner with friends followed. A young couple volunteered the use of a Potter 19 trailer and *Tanbark* was put on it. Then Gary piled into his truck and transported us, man and boat, to the mouth of the Neuse River in North Carolina. On his way home, he called my wife to tell her I was all right—and I was, thanks in no small part to him. Finding unexpected virtue is one of the great joys of travel.

PAMLICO SOUND

Originally, I had hoped to sail *Tanbark* a thousand miles; now I just wanted to look around. A white sky and no wind soon confirmed that the static high was in full effect in the Carolinas as well as Florida. Temperatures were slightly eased, though, and the Neuse River was a welcome change of scene. NOAA's daily litany of thunderstorm warnings carried more weight here, though. By mid-afternoon, thunderstorms were wandering freely around the landscape. After a pleasant night in Oriental, I elected not to follow the waterway channel but to continue up the sound to Kitty Hawk. For anyone with a shoal-draft boat, this is a rewarding option. The winds remained very light but the sound from Swanquarter north was an unspoiled natural expanse of green shoreline unbroken by houses or condos or any signs of man. For two days, I had the place to myself. (Almost.)

There were greenhead flies whom the Lord in His providence sustains by the millions on thin air alone until a sailor happens by. Perhaps my tanbark sails resembled mammoth inverted porkchops (they weren't called "leg-o-mutton" sails for nothing), or perhaps in the heat they could smell me a mile downwind—in any case, they visited in regimental strength. At one point, a furry horse-fly the size of a quarter droned out, hit the mainsail with a wallop, and landed on my arm. I addressed him with a sailor's oath, then smashed him with my free hand. When I removed the hand, he flew out unimpressed, orbited the boat twice, then flew into the cabin, presumably to settle accounts later. Don't go down there without lots of Cutter's and a flyswatter.

Swanquarter gave me an awful night. It was a hot, windless night with no waiting for thunderstorms that couldn't quite get organized. Mosquitoes stalked the cabin, sending emissaries one by one. Suddenly there was a heavy crash against the side of the hull, then another. I flew topside with my flare pistol, ready to repel boarders, but no one was there. Sometime later I was treated to the death struggle of a duck with an alligator or a snapping turtle, replete with howlings and squawkings and wet thrashings, followed by a gurgly silence. It was a long night.

When I arose, I surfaced to see a hand reaching up at me from beneath the hull and what was left of my heart turned over. Then the hand moved free and revealed itself to be a submerged rubber glove with air in the fingers. That particular day ended with a sample of what a fully matured thunderstorm can do. As I was tiptoeing past Gull Rocks, an area to be devoutly avoided, the wind picked up rapidly, then dangerously. A cold gust slapped my back and turned me around and see the sky and seas behind me blacken as a wall of white froth raced across the water and slammed into the rigging. Its rapidity was appalling. Now I was especially glad I'd rigged a jib downhaul, and under bare poles *Tanbark* rode high and dry. Lightning walked around on hot legs and I sat waiting for death in the pouring rain under the only mast on the horizon. It was no wonder that Martin Luther, under similar circumstances, made a vertical offer that if he were permitted to survive the next twenty minutes or so, he'd do something really neat with the rest of his life.

I pulled into the fishing village of Engelhard, North Carolina to the Big Trout Marina. A man named Loren Jarvis appeared on his porch.

"You don't look too wet," he said. "You come on in." I puddled my way to his phone. His wife fixed me something to drink.

"We watched you come in," she said.

I asked if there was a restaurant nearby and there was, but Mr. Jarvis handed me keys:

"Now you just get yourself a hot shower and dry off good, then take the truck in. Looks like you've already had enough."

And so I had.

The stationary high replaced itself with a stationary low and I found myself once more enjoying the hospitality of southern strangers.

Alva Lee Whitely, almost in his eighties, offered the next day to show me the sights and I learned as we drove about his wife with Alzheimer's disease, how he dressed her each day and put on her jewelry. "She's as beautiful today as she was thirty years ago," he said. He carries her to the car, he told me "when it's nice," for rides, and once a week to the beauty parlor. A love story unfolded as beautiful as any. Surely this too is a sea story, for we voyage to see and then remember not just the ocean things but the land also, and the people we encounter along the way. For we see both the land and the people through a fresh lens when we meet them sailing. That experience, more than miles covered, makes us travelers.

I ended my cruise at Engelhard as the weather remained sour and Loren offered to store *Tanbark* for $2 a day while I fetched my trailer from Cape Cod. I had covered about 500 miles under conditions far different than I had imagined. I'm reminded that a small boat is, after all, small; inlets especially are places to be wary of. My winter dreams had been of adventure; my summer reality had been prudence. The adventures, which are matters of scale anyway, came of their own accord. Most of all, I'll remember the kindness of strangers and their stories.

Getting Information: Atlantic Southeast

National Park Service
Southeast Regional Office
75 Spring Street Southeast
Atlanta, GA 30303
404-331-4998

Virginia Division of Tourism
1021 East Cary Street, 14th Floor
Richmond, VA 23219
804-786-4484

**North Carolina Department of
 Tourism**
430 North Salisbury
Raleigh, NC 27611
919-733-4171

South Carolina Office of Tourism
1205 Pendleton Street
Columbia, SC 29201
803-734-0128

**Georgia Dept. of Industry, Trade,
 and Tourism**
PO Box 1776
Atlanta, GA 30301
404-656-3545

Florida Division of Tourism
126 Van Buren
Tallahassee, FL 32399-2000
904-487-1462

CHAPTER 10

The Gulf Coast

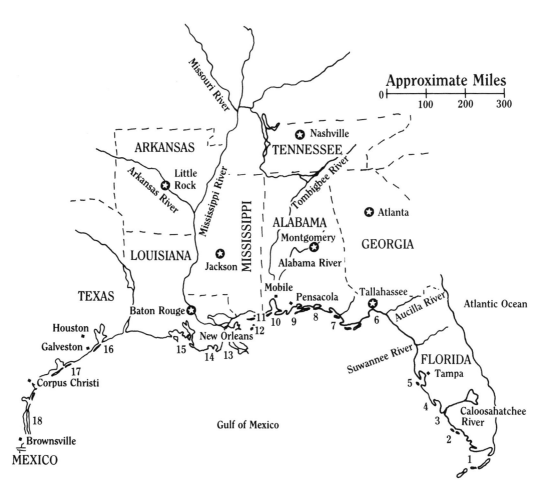

Points of Interest
1. Florida Bay
2. Ten Thousand Islands
3. Pine Island Sound
4. Charlotte Harbor
5. Tampa Bay
6. Apalachee Bay
7. St. George Sound
8. Choctawhatchee Bay
9. Pensacola Bay
10. Mobile Bay
11. Mississippi Sound
12. Chandeleur Sound/ Breton Sound
13. Barataria Bay/Grand Isle
14. Terrebonne Bay
15. Atchafalaya Bay
16. Galveston Bay
17. Matagorda Bay
18. Padre Island/Laguna Madre

THE GULF COAST of the United States is not as well known nationally as are some of the areas we've already looked at, but there's a lot here. In summertime, this area is going to be very hot and humid—especially for people not used to the southern climate—but for people living south of the Mason-Dixon Line, that won't be a problem. For Northerners, the Gulf Coast offers opportunities to sail at times of the year when home waters are frozen or too cold for safety or comfort.

Remember that the fall is hurricane season in these waters. If you plan to sail then, stay well tuned to weather frequencies and do not commit to lengthy voyages along the coast that could catch you in unprotected waters when a storm strikes.

Rivers of the Gulf Coast

WESTERN FLORIDA

For the most part, the rivers of western Florida offer more opportunities to find shelter, charm, and provisions than they offer useful access to the interior. One exception, the Caloosahatchee, connects the Gulf Coast with Lake Okeechobee, which, in turn, connects to the Atlantic Coast. Farther north, the Suwannee River and the Aucilla River in the Panhandle's Apalachee Bay make for interesting pull-in points. The rivers are the least of Florida's many attractions for trailer sailors. Near their mouths, these rivers are suited for **novice** sailors.

MOBILE/TOMBIGBEE RIVERS

The Alabama and the Tombigbee Rivers join to form the Mobile River which, in turn, drains into Mobile Bay. These rivers are part of a network creating a waterway offering opportunities for inland lake sailing and for access to the nation's heartland. A trailer sailor could put in upriver, go with the flow, and end up in Mobile Bay—or even continue with some gulf sailing. Such trips require strategies for reuniting boat and trailer, but they offer opportunities for sampling an interesting variety of waters during a relatively short trip. There is commercial traffic on this waterway, and since big vessels have virtually no room to maneuver, you must stay clear. A hand-held radio can be a godsend here; you can inform

The Tombigbee River has been turned into a major commercial and recreational waterway by the Army Corps of Engineers. Courtesy of the Alabama Bureau of Tourism and Travel.

skippers of your intention to stand clear and get any instructions for your own safety. Channel 16 will get you through. A **novice** with a motor should be fine.

THE MISSISSIPPI RIVER

The Mississippi was called "The Father of Waters." As such, it has much historic and geographical interest. The river is also a *major* artery for heavy commercial traffic. The river continually changes its course, carving out riverbanks and spilling whole trees into its current, which can be very strong. Bucking the current occasions the risk of colliding head-on with 55-gallon drums, trees, or any other heavy-duty flotsam that might be coming your way. I'd suggest that you bypass the river in favor of the whole network of surrounding waterways that make up the Mississippi Delta. You can get all the flavor without the risks. Bays and bayous lace the area, making the delta a fascinating sailing ground—especially for anyone unused to the region. The blend of French, Indian, Black, and Anglo cultures adds lots of Cajun spice to everything. Visit New Orleans for scenery, jazz, and the area's distinctive cuisine. Charts are essential to help you find your way around in the complicated mazes of channels and byways. **Novice,** with motor.

THE INTRACOASTAL WATERWAY

Consider the waterway to be a weird river running parallel to the Gulf, with its current reversing direction in harmony with the tides. The waterway's canals connect all the bays and inshore lakes that run from Florida to Mexico. For our purposes, we'll assume that trailer sailors will be less apt to make tedious canal passages than driving to their specific points of interest and putting in. The *Waterway Guide* for the Gulf Coast offers useful advice for anyone sailing in these waters. Its authors will be the first to insist that it is not intended as a replacement for marine charts of the areas you intend to sail.

Lakes of the Gulf Coast

LAKE PONTCHARTRAIN

You can sail right up to New Orleans by entering Lake Pontchartrain via the Intracoastal Waterway. Urban waterfronts are not always designed to accommodate little boats, and New Orleans is such a place. It makes sense to tie up at yacht basins on either side of the canal leading to the lake and take the bus into town. (Currents can be strong in the passageway.) The lake is deeper along its rim than in its center and strong winds can make anchoring bumpy on the downwind shore. Like shrimp? Try catching your own in the lake. Have garlic and butter on hand.

CLEAR LAKE

Texas's Clear Lake is accessible from the Intracoastal Waterway and a nice way to visit Houston and the nearby space center. Marina facilities are plentiful as are places to eat and other amenities. There's a tremendous concentration of boating in the area, as well as commercial fishing. Ask where the best spots for fishing and shrimping are. As in Pontchartrain, there are good things to be caught—and eaten—here.

All the lakes mentioned that rim the Gulf Coast are manageable by **novice** sailors, provided a wide berth is given to commercial traffic. If you plan to enter or leave lakes that are drained by a single, narrow channel, you'll need more than minimal outboard power. I'd suggest a 500-pound boat have at least a 2 h.p. motor . . . an 800 pound boat have at least a 3 h.p. motor. (A 1,000 boat should have at least a 4 h.p. motor.)

Bays of The Gulf Coast

SAN CARLOS BAY/PINE ISLAND SOUND/CHARLOTTE HARBOR

This trio of pretty bays lies offshore of Fort Myers in southwestern Florida, protected from the surf by Captiva and Sanibel Islands. While deeper-draft boats have to watch their step in places like this, you'll be able to see bottom before you hit it. You can sail in or launch from any number of places, including upriver on the Caloosahatchee. Tides are not as dramatic as in northern waters, but currents can suck you over sand flats and perhaps compel you to stay longer than you might have planned. Start off by staying in the channel, experimenting gradually with excursions off the beaten path until you have a feel for things. Sandy colors can indicate either sand flats or main channels where swift currents drag along a visible cloud of sand in suspension.

TAMPA BAY

Not only is Tampa Bay one of Florida's maritime jewels, it's one of the finest harbors on the continent. Access from the gulf is easy; the bay is surrounded with potential ramp-launching points. Winds tend to be mild; genoas are useful sails here. You've got access to both Tampa and Clearwater's restaurants and shops as well as to superb sailing. Poke into Old Tampa Bay in the northwest corner, swing right behind St. Petersburg's beachfront, or explore the small, sandy keys at the mouth of Pass-A-Grille inlet. If you go barefoot, beware little spherical burrs that dry out and jam into your feet as you cross the crowns of the islands. The beaches are free of them, thank goodness. A **novice** sailor can gain good open-water experience here; families can find something fun for everyone around here. Keep out a weather eye for thunderstorms.

APALACHICOLA BAY

You're off the beaten trail here on Florida's neglected Panhandle. Prices are easy on the wallet; the pace is slow and low key. Barrier islands from Carrabelle to the west of Apalachicola form an attractive sailing spot. A winter visit requires sweaters, but it will seem autumn-like for folks who left the snow and ice behind. Get local advice before venturing from the bay to the Gulf of Mexico.

PENSACOLA BAY

The bay isn't one of Florida's biggest, but it's pretty and it's home to some impressive naval shipping—including the aircraft carrier *Lexington*.

MOBILE BAY

This is Alabama's seaport and the exit point for the Tennessee–Tombigbee Waterway; watch for commercial traffic. The bay can get up a nasty chop when the winds are brisk. This might be best considered a **mariner**'s location. What's the attraction? It's Mobile—a city rich in multinational history, architecture, and cuisine. This is the *south!* Imagine walking back to your boat under the spread of huge trees dripping with Spanish moss.

MISSISSIPPI SOUND

The Gulf Coast west of Mobile is protected by a string of barrier islands. They are objects of interest, as are the seaports on the mainland. Biloxi is particularly charming. Once you free yourself from commercial traffic, here and the following two bays are good places for **novices.**

GALVESTON BAY

Galveston Bay is a good-sized body of water. The shoreline can be swampy and, if strong northerlies blow some of the water out of the bay, you'll get to stay on it longer than you planned. (Many of the Gulf's bays are quite shallow. Strong offshore winds can blow sufficient water out of the bays to ground your boat. This happened to us off Tampa Bay and could happen to you elsewhere.) Galveston Bay is less than 10 feet deep almost everywhere.

LAGUNA MADRE

This bay is formed by the extensive barrier islands along the Mexican coast south of the Texas border. Much of the surrounding land is rolling dunes and a wildlife refuge. You'll need a shoal-draft boat to negotiate the thin waters outside the waterway channel, but this could be a satisfying wilderness trip, taken at a slow pace.

Coastal Cruising Along the Gulf

Much of the Gulf of Mexico is shallow and subject to very rough sea conditions during periods of high winds. Still, parts of the coast lend themselves to leisurely exploration. If you're planning any ambitious coasting trips along the gulf (or along any coastline, really), leave an itinerary called a "float plan" with friends with a promise to call them upon your safe arrival. If you fail to call, they can give the Coast Guard your intended route.

FLORIDA'S TEN THOUSAND ISLANDS SHORELINE

The Ten Thousand Islands near Everglades City form a natural maze of largely untouched islands through which you can do some wilderness sailing. This is tropical sailing: Prepare for bugs with effective screening. This would be an effective location for a **novice** sailor to alternate sailing inside and outside safely in a fascinating setting.

TARPON SPRINGS

Greek sponge fishermen settled this Florida harbor and left a distinctive cultural and architectural mark. In fair weather, this could make a good

passage for someone new to coastal sailing. You could sail from Tampa Bay and head right up the coast. It's about 45 miles, depending on where you put in. Take a bus back to retrieve your car and trailer.

CHANDELEUR SOUND/ISLAND

The Mississippi delta is continuously being formed by the thousands of tons of soil and debris the river carries and then drops as the river hits the gulf and loses its velocity. The whole area would make an interesting place to snoop around in a small boat. The Chandeleur Sound is particularly interesting, since the Chandeleur islands provide shelter from the gulf. Check out Chandeleur Island and Grand Isle in Barataria Bay across the delta. Terrebonne Bay, Atchafalaya Bay, and Vermilion Bay, with the Russell Sage and Shell Keys wildlife refuges are additional points of interest.

Getting Information: Gulf Coast

Mississippi Dept. of Economic and Community Development
Tourism Division
PO Box 849
Jackson, MS 39205
601-359-3414

Alabama Dept. of Tourism and Travel
532 South Perry Street
Montgomery, AL 36104-4614
205-242-4169

Louisiana Office of Tourism
PO Box 94291
Department 324
Baton Rouge, LA 70804
504-342-8119

Texas Department of Commerce
Tourism Division
PO Box 12008
Austin, TX 78711
512-462-9191

CHAPTER 11

The Greater Lakes Region

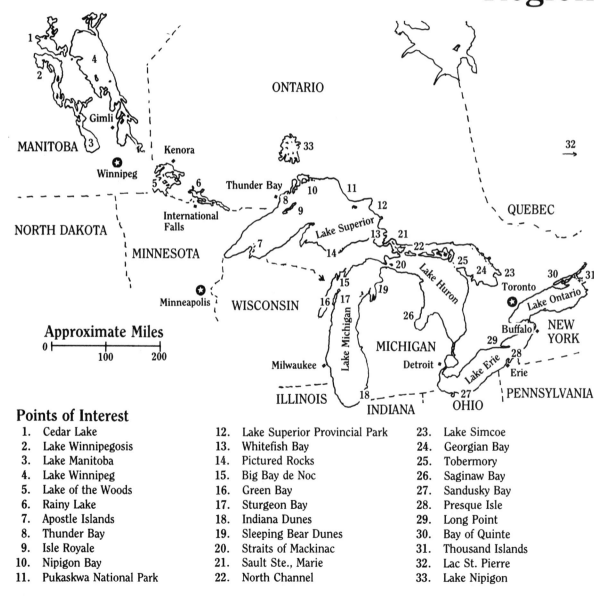

Points of Interest

1. Cedar Lake
2. Lake Winnipegosis
3. Lake Manitoba
4. Lake Winnipeg
5. Lake of the Woods
6. Rainy Lake
7. Apostle Islands
8. Thunder Bay
9. Isle Royale
10. Nipigon Bay
11. Pukaskwa National Park
12. Lake Superior Provincial Park
13. Whitefish Bay
14. Pictured Rocks
15. Big Bay de Noc
16. Green Bay
17. Sturgeon Bay
18. Indiana Dunes
19. Sleeping Bear Dunes
20. Straits of Mackinac
21. Sault Ste., Marie
22. North Channel
23. Lake Simcoe
24. Georgian Bay
25. Tobermory
26. Saginaw Bay
27. Sandusky Bay
28. Presque Isle
29. Long Point
30. Bay of Quinte
31. Thousand Islands
32. Lac St. Pierre
33. Lake Nipigon

WHEN THE LAST great glaciers retreated at the end of the most recent Ice Age, they left thousands of lakes in their wake. Several of these are the largest freshwater lakes in the world. We call lakes Superior, Michigan, Huron, Erie, and Ontario the Great Lakes, and forget that not far away to the north are several others almost as big: Winnipeg and the Manitoba/Winnipegosis system. Looking at the region geographically and not politically, we'll refer to this area as the *Greater Lakes* region. Since there are numerous smaller lakes strewn about with a lavish hand, we'll look at the largest of these too.

While the shallower lakes of Manitoba warm up a bit in the summer, the larger lakes are very cold—usually not more than 45 degrees Fahrenheit even in summer. This requires great caution on your part. You have about 15 minutes after a capsize or a fall overboard or the effects of lost body heat will begin to set in, soon making any further efforts worthless. Children lose their body heat more rapidly. Hypothermia is a real hazard here. Obviously there is a lot of boating going on in the Greater Lakes; you'll just have to take care.

The Great Lakes are vast, oceanic bodies of fresh water. Consider crossing one of these in a small boat in the same way you'd consider an offshore ocean passage. The lakes have been known to whip up monstrous storms with almost impossible sea conditions. The popular song *The Wreck of the Edmund Fitzgerald* memorializes the loss of a 729-foot, well-found ore carrier, "the pride of the American side." I would consider a Great Lake crossing to be an **expert** proposition, to be undertaken with a wet suit or survival suit for all hands in a boat equipped for ocean voyaging. Lake bottoms are often rock; a grapnel makes a good second anchor. Treat these bodies of water with great respect.

For most small-boat sailors, this area offers a dazzling wealth of beautiful scenery and good, breezy sailing. The nooks and crannies of these big lakes create ideal sailing grounds. Often you'll find these areas sprinkled with islands and blessed with an occasional sandy beach. The waters are usually very clean. What more could you want?

Sailing Canada's Greater Lakes

The first big lake we come across as we head across the northern prairie is Manitoba's Cedar Lake. It's a big open lake, about 35 miles long by 20 miles wide. The town of Easterville is close by for shoreside support.

To the south of Cedar Lake is Lake Winnipegosis, a 140-mile-long wilderness lake that's about 20 miles across at its wider points. This is another ideal spot for sailing, with numerous islands and coves along the lake's length. There are several towns up there that offer shoreside support and serve as jump-off points: Camperville, Duck Bay, Overflowing River, and the town of Winnipegosis on the lake's southwest shore. You'll have to be completely self-sufficient if you plan to venture far up there.

Not far to the southeast of Lake Winnipegosis is the first of the really big lakes: Lake Manitoba, spreading some 1,800 square miles with a length of about 120 miles and a varied width. About 50 miles up the lake the east and west shores pinch in, forming an upper lake with a wealth of coves and bays. Shorelines can be boggy, so be sure your mosquito netting has no tears, and bring your bug repellent. You'll need both.

Lake Manitoba has one particular oddity: It's quite shallow in parts. While this means anchoring won't be much of a problem, it also means that in high winds Manitoba can whip up a phenominal chop.

Even the southern shore of Lake Manitoba is very rural. I had trouble finding my way to the water's edge. After blundering to a shoreline road, I stopped at a house, rang the bell, and was greeted by a friendly fellow who spread a chart across his kitchen table and told me a bit about the place. Fairweather winds are most apt to be out of the west. Ramps are not fancy affairs, local fishermen use them, mostly. Lake Manitoba's appeal stems from really getting away from the crowd. On a sailboat, you'll be an oddity. I stood in this man's backyard and the lake spead out vast and empty. It was almost odd. As I was eager to reach Lake Winnipeg to the northeast before dark, I didn't go searching for a ramp, besides it was about to rain. Time permitting, I would have headed for the upper lake. There the land would be less featureless and the sailing more interesting.

The 270-mile-long Lake Winnipeg is the biggest of the Manitoba lakes, covering 9,400 square miles. It's just a little smaller than Lake Erie and actually bigger than one of the "great" lakes, Lake Ontario. It has more miles of shoreline to it than all the Great Lakes except Superior. Like Manitoba, it is pinched almost in two about 50 miles up. The narrows at Hecla Provincial Park are a compelling place to explore. The next 30 miles or so are full of islands and coves. At its maximum width, the lake flares out to 30 miles. When I sailed out of Gimli on the southwestern shore, it was like sailing into an ocean with tan, sand-colored water. *Fearless* rode rollers that were the biggest I found on the trip except for the Pacific. You can't see across anything nearly this big, especially since the surrounding countryside is flat.

There are a number of towns along the southern shoreline. If you go all the way to the northern end, there's a sheltered harbor at Limestone Point Bay. The city of Winnipeg is close by the south end; you can find anything you need there. The Canadians do cities very well; urban planners from the U.S. could do worse than visit Victoria and Calgary, just to see how simple it appears to be to keep things clean and open.

As you drive farther east along the Trans-Canada highway, you enter Ontario's lake country. There are thousands of lakes of all sizes in Ontario. For wilderness sailing in a trailerable boat, Lake of the Woods, a maze of coves and islands covering an area of approximately 50 by 60 miles, is superb. The town of Kenora on the lake's northwest shore would be a good place to start. Bring screens and bug repellent, especially for the southern end of the lake.

If you've got a sailing canoe, you might especially enjoy Rainy Lake or Quetico Provincial Park, Ontario. It's a rough 40-mile by 10-mile expanse of islands, coves and waterways. The park can provide a base camp for a jump to the nearby towns of Island View and International Falls, Minnesota. There is a second park on the southern side of the lake: Voyageurs National Park.

Just north of Thunder Bay, Ontario lies Lake Nipigon, with its own provincial park. It's about the same size as Lake of the Woods, but it has more open water. Ontario has many other lakes, Lake Nipissing in north central Ontario being the largest not already mentioned. The lakes of Ontario and Minnesota are among the best for canoeing in either country. The larger sporting goods stores and wilderness outfitters can help you lay out a trip that can, with occasional portages, take you through a string of lakes. Personally, I'd adapt my canoe for oar power and mount a simple sailing rig. But then I'm not an experienced paddler and there must be something about it I've failed to appreciate.

The province of Quebec has Lake St. Jean, a roughly 20-mile by 25-mile sailing ground near Pointe Taillon Provincial Park. Its good sailing lures people up from Quebec City to vacation here. From St. Jean, the Saguenay River flows to join the St. Lawrence, cutting its way through the only real fjord in North America. It's a spectacular place.

A **novice** sailor could do some pleasant sailing on any of the lakes we've mentioned so far. I'd consider Winnipeg, Winnipegosis, and Manitoba **mariner** class bodies of water if a sailor intended to stay a week or more out of touch with civilization—or if someone intended to navigate their greatest length or breadth. If someone wanted to exercise some passagemaking ambitions in this part of the continent, there are worse places then Lake Winnipeg's southern end.

Sailing the Great Lakes

For most trailer sailors, long passagemaking in these lakes is unnecessary. If I were warming up for an ocean passage, a voyage across Superior or Michigan (which can get unbelievably nasty) might be a good shakedown. I'd have a wet suit or a survival suit and a boat set up for ocean conditions. For family sailing, there are so many worthwhile places to explore, it could take *years,* even taking advantage of the highways between attractions. I've focused here on national, provincial, and state parks. There, you'll find the parking, ramps, and facilities you'll need—and your kids are apt to find companions their own age to hang out with.

There's a fascinating area in western Lake Superior called the Apostle Islands National Lakeshore, a 30-mile by 30-mile haven of islands, big and

All day and night the trains rumble in, packed with the wheat harvest of the Canadian plains. These huge silos, filled to the brim, load a steady stream of Great Lakes grain ships. Quite a spectacle.

little—a perfect sheltered cruising ground. Visit Big Bay State Park in Madeline Island. The Wisconsin towns of Ashland, Washburn, Bayfield, Red Cliff, and Cornucopia can serve as shoreside supports. The best way to sample Superior's delights (and the other big lakes) is from locations where shelter is available quickly if conditions deteriorate.

Thunder Bay, Ontario on Lake Superior is the site of one of Canada's two major grain exporting centers. Huge dockside silos, fed by continuous rail traffic from the prairie provinces, discharge grain onto freighters day and night. There's a good municipal marina here with launching facilities near places to eat and a homemade ice cream store. This is an interesting place to poke around. A huge peninsula takes the shallow form of a supine Indian—"the Sleeping Giant," which protects Thunder Bay from Superior's storms. Sibley Provincial Park forms one corner of the bay; Pie Island is off the harbor's mouth.

After my return home from our round-the-continent trip, a letter was waiting from the harbormaster of Thunder Bay, hoping my stay was a pleasant one and that the rest of my trip was safe and productive. It was a gracious letter and the only one of its kind I received. Some 30 miles offshore is Isle Royale, a 45-mile-long rocky island and national park. Rock Harbor sits at the northeast end and provides the island's only marina. It would make a nice passage on a well-behaved but breezy day. In a small and slower boat, I'd launch in the municipal marina and sail out to the giant, anchor overnight at Sibley Park, visit Pie Island and return the next day.

To the east of Thunder Bay is a series of interesting sailing locations: Black Bay, around the corner from the Sleeping Giant, and then Nipigon Bay and Terrace Bay, with a string of islands close to shore. The shoreline is bold and rocky with forests running right down to the water. The water is 45 degrees, so a quick plunge over the side is about all you'll be able to stand. Use a Solar Shower to get a warm soaking while you lather up, then a quick howling plunge to rinse off.

Continuing around the northern rim of Superior, you'll find Puckaskwa National Park and Lake Superior Provincial Park. Camping should be ideal with bracing breezes coming off the lake, even in hot weather. Offshore is Michipicoten Island—about at the midpoint between the two parks. There's a little cove in the middle of the island's south shore. Get local charts before cruising to the island, or anywhere on this unforgiving lake. Most shorelines are rocky and unforgiving. Charts, a grapnel anchor, and a weather radio are vital for cruising any of the Great Lakes.

On the south shore of Superior lies Michigan's Pictured Rocks National Lakeshore. Grand Isle and other islands are close to shore; the Hiawatha National Forest is just inland too.

As Lake Superior narrows on its way into Lake Huron, you enter the interesting Sault Ste. Marie area. Ontario is to your north; Michigan is to your south. You can explore Superior's Whitefish Bay and Tahquamenon State Park. Michigan's Paradise and Emerson are towns close to the western shore, setting-off points for the numerous islands around: St. Joseph, Drummond, and Cockburn—and numerous channels and bays. Be mindful that commercial traffic headed for the St. Lawrence Seaway must be given a wide berth. As you continue east, you arrive at still another delight.

Lake Huron's North Channel formed by Manitoulin and Cockburn Island is considered to be one of the world's prime cruising grounds. A series of large islands protect the North Channel from the lake itself, and the whole area is laced with islands and coves. Small-boat sailors can spend the first half of their vacation happily getting lost in this maze of waterways, then spend the second half reluctantly finding their way out again. Grapnel hooks are useful here to anchor amid rocks where a Danforth would skate along the bottom. Bring a second line to lead to shore and tie around a tree; rig the ropes to suspend you in the middle of a little hollow too small for a big boat to even look at. The prevailing summer wind is westerly.

You can save time by taking to the highways. At the end of the channel is Georgian Bay, almost another Great Lake all by itself. The bay's north shoreline offers more nooks and crannies. Parry Sound, about one-third of the way along the coast, might be a good starting point if you want to sample the bay. Or you can visit Georgian Bay Islands National Park, with islands spread across a large part of the bay.

After North Channel, try exploring Manitoulin Island. The town of Little Current has an endless town pier for docking. There's a ramp nearby, should you want to begin or end a trip there. At the southeast end of the island is a ferry service that can take your car and boat to Tobermory across Huron at the tip of the Bruce Peninsula. There's an underwater marine park in Tobermory where you can dive to submerged wrecks 12 to 20 feet down. The water is 45 degrees, so for more than a quick plunge, I'd recommend a wet suit. The water is clear to 30 feet and clean enough to drink; I just dipped my cup over the side. The whole area has the rocky feel of the Maine coast—but without the tides.

From here, you can head down into the lower portion of Huron or bear northwest to Lake Michigan. Let's take a look at one more Huron attraction before changing lakes. Michigan extends northward like an upraised mitten on a giant left hand. The body of water contained inside the thumb is Saginaw Bay—a most pleasant spot covering an area roughly 50 miles by 20 miles. There are some sandy beaches here and often good breezes. You can start at Bay City State Park or visit Wild Fowl Bay and explore some islands off the bay's eastern shore.

To enter Lake Michigan from Lake Huron requires negotiating the interesting Straits of Mackinac. The narrow channel is sprinkled with attractive, charming islands, Mackinac Island, Bois Blanc Island, Cheboygan State Park. On the Lake Michigan side are the Michigan Islands Wildlife Refuge and still more islands, Beaver Island being the largest.

Down Lake Michigan's east coast lies Sleeping Bear Dunes National Lakeshore. This is a place the kids will love. North and South Manitou Islands are offshore within two to three hours sail. Traverse City is nearby for shoreside support.

The lake's south shore is thickly settled with Chicago and Gary, Indiana. Northeast of Gary is Indiana Dunes National Lakeshore. The town of Dune Acres is close by.

The waters of Lake Huron near Tobermory on the Bruce Peninsula are clear to 30 feet. You can dive to sunken wrecks at an underwater marine park. Take care, though, the water is frigid.

A stiff breeze fills the sails of some participants in the Lake Erie Wooden Sailboat Regatta off Sandusky. Courtesy of Erie County (Ohio) Chamber of Commerce.

Across the lake in Wisconsin from Sleeping Bear Dunes National Lakeshore is Green Bay, both the 70-mile by 15-mile body of water and the city. Sturgeon Bay, about halfway up the Door Peninsula that forms Green Bay is an inviting area to explore. At the northern end of Green Bay is Big Bay de Noc, a 200-square-mile sailing ground with access to both the Hiawatha National Forest and Fayette State Park. The passage from Lake Huron down into Lake Erie is heavily industrialized. Here I wouldn't dip my cup down to drink; this is no playground for small boats.

Lake Erie, approximately 240 miles by 60 miles, is shallower than the others and can be whipped into a nasty chop more readily. Its waters aren't so cold, though. In past years, Erie had a reputation for pollution, and ecologists worried that the lake would take at least a century to recover. Industrial compassion (inspired by federal legislation) has seen a resurgence of the lake's natural vigor well ahead of the worst forecasts.

Ohio's Sandusky Bay is a popular spot for sailors, and the western lake is scattered with offshore islands. Three islands have state parks on them: Kellys, South Bass (popularly called "Put-in Bay"), and Catawba. The city of Sandusky has an amusement park that might interest the kids.

A spot of interest on Erie's eastern end is Presque Isle State Park, a tranquil peninsula off Erie, Pennsylvania. From here an adventurous mariner might undertake a 30-mile passage across the lake to Long Point on the Canadian shore. At the base of the Long Point peninsula is Port Rowan, Ontario. Check your forecast.

For larger vessels, the Welland Canal connects Lake Erie with Lake Ontario. But why bother? Drive around and visit Niagara Falls on your way. The eastern end of the lake can be congested with commercial traffic; it's no playground for small boats. Lake Ontario is the smallest of the Great Lakes, only one quarter the size of Superior. The Bay of Quinte on the northeast side of the lake is a very pretty 40-mile winding channel. The town of Belleville is a great stopping point.

At the head of the lake, the Thousand Islands area (discussed in the Middle Atlantic States) provides a small-boat paradise all its own.

Getting Information: The Greater Lakes

National Park Service
Midwest Regional Office
1709 Jackson Street
Omaha, NE 68102
402-221-3448

Indiana Tourism Division
One North Capitol
Suite 7000
Indianapolis, IN 46204
317-232-8860

Iowa Department of Economic Development
200 East Grand
Des Moines, IA 50316
515-281-3100

Illinois Office of Tourism
310 South Michigan Avenue
Suite 108
Chicago, IL 60604
312-793-2094

Wisconsin Division of Tourism
PO Box 7606
Madison, WI 53707
608-266-2161

Michigan Bureau of Tourism
333 South Capitol Street
Suite F
Lansing, MI 48933
517-373-1195

Minnesota Office of Tourism
375 Jackson
Room 250
St. Paul, MN 55101
612-296-5029

Ontario Ministry of Tourism and Recreation
Customer Sales and Service
9th Floor
77 Bloor Street West
Toronto
Ontario M7A 2R5 CANADA
416-965-4008

Travel Manitoba
7th Floor
155 Carlton Street
Winnipeg
Manitoba, R3C 3H8 CANADA
204-945-3777

Ohio Division and Travel and Tourism
P.O. Box 1001
Columbus, OH 43266-0101
1-800-BUCKEYE
(800-282-5393)

CHAPTER 12

Sailing Middle America

Points of Interest

1. North Saskatchewan River
2. Last Mountain Lake
3. Lake Diefenbaker
4. Ft. Peck Lake
5. Lake Sakakawea
6. Lake Oahe
7. Lake Francis Case
8. Winnibigoshish Lake
9. Leech Lake
10. Lake Winnebago
11. Rathbun Lake
12. Tuttle Creek Lake
13. Lake O' The Cherokees
14. Eufaula Reservoir
15. Amistad Reservoir
16. Sam Rayburn Lake
17. Toledo Bend Reservoir
18. Kentuck Lake/Lake Barkley
19. Lake Cumberland
20. Table Rock and
    Bull Shoals Lakes
21. Watts Bar Lake system
22. Wilson Lake
23. Wheeler Lake

THE INTERIOR OF the continent is laced with a network of rivers. Several of these, like the Missouri, have very scenic stretches. One can travel the Missouri for hundreds of miles, or follow tributaries down to the Mississippi and continue on to the Gulf of Mexico. I worry about waterways downstream of major industrial areas and large cities. The water may be too foul to swim in—let alone to drink—since some contaminants can be absorbed directly into the skin. Bottom dwellers in the Mississippi, including the famous catfish—a Mark Twain delicacy—are living in river bottoms layered with industrial and agricultural toxins.

The waterways south of major cities are busy commercial arteries, plied by freighters and strings of mammoth barges. I'm frankly not sure that the heavily-trafficked stretches of the river are suitable places for small sailboats with limited horsepower and hull speeds. More pastoral stretches exist, of course, but when you see the array of attractive lakes laid out by the Army Corps of Engineers, you'll know that the rivers need only be used if you've selected a river trip because you *prefer* river traveling.

The Lakes of Middle America

If you live in the continent's heartland there's at least one lake within a hundred miles of your door—almost without exception. Especially in flat country, you can expect good wind on most days. In pioneer times, the continuous moaning of the wind drove some settlers over the edge of madness. For you, that wind means the rattle of canvas and the gurgle of water under your hull.

For most days, these lakes are within the skill range of **novice** sailors. Listen for weather reports—especially in tornado country. If river passages appeal to you, I'd stick to the pastoral stretches above urban effluents and heavy commercial traffic. Most sailors living on either coast have no idea of the sailing opportunities available to "flatlanders" in the middle of the continent. The land we're calling Middle America lies between the Appalachian Mountains in the East and the Rocky Mountains in the West—a relatively flat expanse drained by many rivers. Both the Canadian and American governments have erected scores of dams along these rivers, generating hydroelectric power and creating recreational lakes for the whole interior of the continent. We'll proceed state by state, but first, let's look at the Canadian province of Saskatchewan, where there are three lakes of interest.

SASKATCHEWAN'S LAKES

A 100-mile lake-like stretch of the Saskatchewan River, including Tobin Lake, is buffeted by dependable prairie winds and makes a great sailing expanse. The towns of Prince Albert and Nipawin offer local amenities. The 75-mile-long Lake Diefenbaker is more rural, with no shorefront urban development. Fifty miles north of the capital city Regina is the third of the province's prairie lakes—the 50-mile Last Mountain Lake. When I drove across the Canadian prairie, people warned me about boredom. To my surprise, though, I liked it. There were interesting subtleties to the landscape and an absence of the institutionalized sameness of our interstate highway facilities. Restaurants were family concerns unhurriedly serving home recipes.

MIDDLE AMERICAN LAKES OF THE U.S.

Here I'll try to cover lakes of 25 miles or longer. Lakes are hard things to measure if they are crooked or have multiple branches, so I'll approximate. How far up a river channel do you measure a lake? We'll look for a major increase in channel width.

Compared with the Rocky Mountain or desert lakes, the Middle American lakes won't usually have the same breathtaking scenery. Without saying they're interchangeable—because they aren't—it makes sense to look for the ones closest to you if time or budget doesn't permit distant travel. What *do* you get at the Middle American lakes? You often get superb sailing breezes. When the winds can blow unobstructed across miles and miles of flatland, you can bet your sails will be filled most days. Most of the lakes we'll be looking at were constructed by the Army Corps of Engineers. In other words, they are *planned* lakes. Count on good access, proper launch ramps, parking spaces, and usually campgrounds, state parks, or recreational areas along the shorefront. You can usually count on reasonably clean water too. If the view along the horizon doesn't bring tears to your eyes, things will be clean and wooded. Huge numbers of families get to heal their damaged bodies and souls by camping, sailing, and soaking their heads in this system of recreational areas.

Four lakes form a spectacular opportunity for open-water sailing in the heart of the continent:

Eastern Montana. The Missouri River has some marvelous scenery of its own. A big dam creates Fort Peck Lake. It's one of the nation's biggest, over 100 miles long and cut with canyons to snoop in.

North Dakota. The Missouri creates another even bigger lake here—almost 150 miles long. Lake Sakakawea has lots of twists and turns to it. Four Bears Recreational Area lies along its banks—as do Lake Sakakawea and Fort Stevenson State Parks. Fort Union Trading Post is nearby.

South Dakota. A dammed Missouri forms Lake Oahe, with its head at North Dakota's capital, Bismark, and its foot at South Dakota's capital, Pierre. It's even longer than Lake Sakakawea. There's a state recreational area on its banks in South Dakota.

South of Pierre, a fourth lake, Lake Francis Case, offers still more sailing opportunities.

Iowa. The state has two lakes, worth checking out, though they are smaller than the giants we've just discussed. Red Rock Lake on the Des Moines River has its head just southeast of Des Moines. You can combine sailing with more urban amusements here. About 50 miles southeast of Des Moines is Rathbun Lake. Both lakes are around 15 miles in length.

Kansas. Ten miles from the Manhattan in northwestern Kansas the Tuttle Creek Reservoir extends some 30 miles.

Nebraska. As part of the Lewis and Clark State Recreation Area on the South Dakota-Nebraska border, Lewis and Clark Lake covers around 60 miles. Facilities there are very good.

Missouri. Near Jefferson City in central Missouri lies Lake of the Ozarks. It's about 25 miles long, with a state park and the town of Osage Beach for shoreside supports. Table Rock Lake on the southern border south of Springfield in the Mark Twain State Forest. The Harry S. Truman Reservoir, 60 miles southeast of Independence and a western arm of the Lake of the Ozarks, has a bush-like structure, offering dozens of waterways to explore.

Oklahoma. About 50 miles east of Tulsa on the Ozark Plateau is the Lake O' the Cherokees with three state recreational areas along its banks. Fifty miles south of Tulsa is Eufaula Reservoir. Fountainhead and Arrowhead State Parks lie along the banks of this big lake. Lake Texoma, almost 50 miles long, is about as big as Eufaula with a state park along its shores too. It's a border lake, about 70 miles north of Dallas-Fort Worth area.

Texas. About 100 miles northeast of Houston, the Sam Rayburn Reservoir stretches out over some 45 miles. Cassels Bend State Recreation Area is there also. The wider Toledo Bend Reservoir covers some 65 miles of the Texas-Louisiana border. Texas has another large lake along its border with Mexico—the Amistad Reservoir; it's about 45 miles long with its own recreational area.

Kentucky. The 45-mile-long Lake Cumberland in south-central Kentucky sits to the west of the Daniel Boone National Forest. The towns of Russell Springs and Burnside are near its banks and provide shoreside support. The Tennessee Valley Authority created two huge lakes with a sprawling recreational area called The Land Between the Lakes located (as you might guess) between them. Kentucky Lake in the state's southwest corner lays claim to being the largest artificial lake in the U.S. Claims vary, depending on whether they're based on total shoreline, area, or maximum length. The lake is big enough to swallow you and your family in bucolic splendor. Nearby Lake Barkley is about 50 miles long; both are

Boat camping on the shores of Kentucky Lake. Courtesy of the Kentucky Department of Tourism.

approximately 75 miles northwest of Nashville, Tennessee. Ramps and camps abound.

Warning: Ticks here can carry Rocky Mountain Spotted Fever and the usual bug sprays don't work; buy *local tick repellent*.

Tennessee. Some 20 miles north of Knoxville is 25-mile-long Norris Lake and state park. The lake has a raggedy Y shape, offering more shoreline than you'd guess. A number of lakes created by dams on the Tennessee River run southwest from Knoxville like a string of pearls: Fort Loudon Lake, Watts Bar Lake, and Chickamauga Lake.

Alabama. Alabama has two lakes whose wandering branches offer pleasant exploring diversions. Both are about 25 miles across: Martin Lake is 25 miles northeast of Montgomery; Lewis Smith Lake is some 30 miles north of Birmingham. Guntersville Lake and Wheeler Lake to the southeast and southwest of Huntsville, respectively are part of the Tennessee River system. Dams on the Chattahoochee River have produced Walter F. George Reservoir and West Point Lake along the Alabama-Georgia state line. Lakepoint Resort State Park provides an added advantage to the Walter George Reservoir.

Georgia. The W-shaped Lake Seminole sits in the southwest corner of the state. Formed by the Flint and the Chattahoochee Rivers, it's about 30 miles across. Clarks Hill Lake northwest of Augusta is bigger, around 60 miles long. Mistletoe and Elijah Clark Memorial State Parks are on its shores.

Virginia and North Carolina. On the two states' border near Clarkesville, Virginia is the 60-mile John H. Kerr Reservoir (Biggs Island Lake), which touches both the Staunton River and the Occoneechee State Parks in Virginia.

Mississippi. The Ross Barnett Reservoir just outside Jackson extends 20 pleasant miles.

National Park Service
Midwest Regional Office
1709 Jackson Street
Omaha, NE 68102
402-221-3448

West Virginia Travel and Tourism Division
West Virginia Division of
  Commerce
2101 Washington Street East
Charleston, WV 25305
304-348-2200

Arkansas Department of Parks and Tourism
One Capitol Mall
Little Rock, AR 72201
501-682-7777

Tennessee Tourism Department
PO Box 23170
Nashville, TN 37202
615-741-2158

Kentucky Department of Travel Development
Capitol Plaza Tower
Frankfort, KY 40601
1-800-225-8747

Missouri Division of Tourism
PO Box 1055
Jefferson City, MO 65102
816-861-8800

Oklahoma State Department of Tourism and Recreation
Literature Distribution
PO Box 60000
Oklahoma City, OK 73146
1-800-652-6552

North Dakota Tourism
Liberty Memorial Building
604 East Boulevard
Bismark, ND 58505
701-224-2525

South Dakota Department of Tourism
Capitol Lake Plaza
Pierre, SD 57501
1-800-843-1930

Saskatchewan Dept. of Economic Development and Tourism
1919 Saskatchewan Drive
Regina
Saskatchewan S4P 3V7 CANADA
1-800-667-7191

CHAPTER **13**

The Desert Lakes

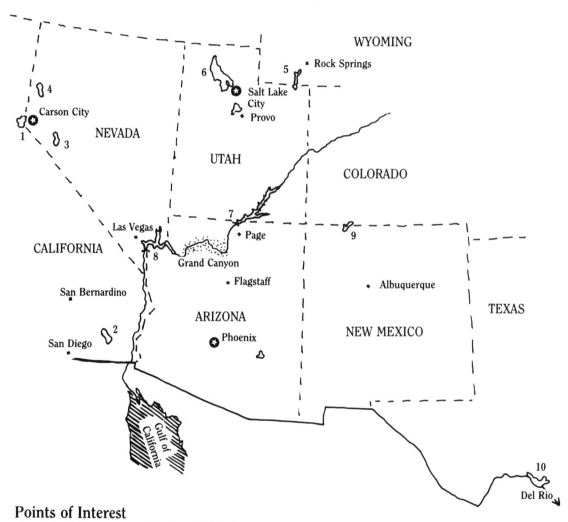

Points of Interest

1. Lake Tahoe
2. Salton Sea
3. Walker Lake
4. Pyramid Lake
5. Flaming Gorge
6. Great Salt Lake
7. Lake Powell
8. Lake Mead
9. Navajo Lake
10. Amistad Reservoir

Approximate Miles

0   100   200

"DESERT LAKES" SOUNDS almost like an oxymoron—a self-contradiction—but thanks to some tremendous hydroelectric dams, the one or two natural lakes of the region have been joined by two huge artificial lakes: Lake Mead and Lake Powell. Sailing on the desert lakes is like sailing on another planet. Weirdly colored rock formations (which change as the sun makes its transit) run down to the water. The land and the water look as if they don't belong together—which they really don't, naturally speaking. Often there is no plant life and, if the powerboats don't come around, there's no suggestion that life has yet begun on Earth. Your boat could as easily be a spaceship. The huge, silent rock formations seem to contain a spiritual presence that suggests you are not as alone as it seems.

The water is clean and just cool enough to offer relief and warm enough to let you soak up to your nostrils as long as you like. Little bugs live in the sandstone and come zooming out at night, but they're not the bloodsucking pests that infest both the tropics and the north. (There are snakes, though.) We're talking, in short, about some of America's prime small-boat country.

For all the lakes of the desert states, you need to be mindful of the effect of the strong Southwest sunlight—which is even more powerful in higher elevations. Because the air may be cooler in the higher elevations, you may not realize the need to take precautions until you've given yourself a serious burn.

Heat and solar effects notwithstanding, this region is a prime vacation ground. Especially for Easterners, this area feels really *different* in a satisfying sort of way. For the same reason, I'd urge a family from the western states, if time and funds permitted, to go to Cape Cod, say, leaving all the familiar things of home far behind.

Every one of these lakes would be a safe place for **novice** sailors to develop their skills and be treated to incredible natural beauty, and because of the natural beauty, even an expert sailor could enjoy the mostly laid-back sailing because being there is the main point anyway.

Man-Made Lakes

LAKE POWELL

Glen Canyon Dam in north-central Arizona blocks the path of the Colorado River north of the Grand Canyon, flooding the main channel and the hundreds of byways and canyons that lead into it. Seen from above, Lake Powell, which runs well into Utah, resembles a defoliated tree. Unlike eastern rivers, the Colorado has no other streams leading into it; it runs through parched country and seems to have little impact on the vegetation near it; the desert stretches to the water's edge.

North of the dam, the Wahweap campground area boasts several of the most impressive launch ramps we saw anywhere in the continent. One area alone had more than 15 lanes leading into the water. Marinas, laundries, restaurants, and a gas station take care of most shoreside needs. Such a wealth of facilities suggests intensive use—and that's the case. On weekends, a steady stream of cars, most of them towing motorboats, flows up and back from Phoenix. If you can explore this lake during the week, you'll find a lot more serenity, and the waters will be safer too.

We set up camp on a sandy Lake Powell beach. You'll need two anchors to keep yourself off the beach and facing the waves.

The best strategy is to explore places from Monday through Thursday or Friday. Then pull out and point yourself for your next destination, smiling in a somewhat superior way at the flood of traffic lined bumper to bumper in the opposite lane, headed into the place you just left.

There are few sailboats on Lake Powell. Winds can be unpredictable—off again, on again. If you carry a motor, it doesn't have to be a high-powered thing, just an easy kicker to burble you along when the wind dies. You could spend a whole vacation on the lake, working your way north to the Rainbow Bridge, exploring whatever canyons appeal to you, photographing awesome scenery. You'll be passed by powerboats that can gobble up a week's worth of sailing miles in a few hours. More power to them, I suppose.

LAKE MEAD

To the west of the Grand Canyon, Nevada's Hoover Dam creates another huge desert lake, Lake Mead. It is broader than Lake Powell and has more room for a sailboat, though it is without the intricate little canyons Lake Powell's convoluted shoreline creates. Lake Mead offers variations on the Powell theme: delightful water, and scenic grandeur. Temple Bar Marina, on the lake's south shore, is an ideal starting point. In both lakes, keep an eye out for thunderstorms. Nearby Las Vegas is worth a visit. If there is a single place in the world where neon has been elevated to an art form, Las Vegas is it.

A visit to this area also would be incomplete without a visit to the Grand Canyon. A scenic highway runs along much of its south rim. Campground space may be limited or nonexistent if you arrive too late in the evening. (We slept caravan-style in a rest stop.) Get a copy of Grofe's classic *Grande Canyon Suite* for your tape deck. It'll get you into the mood nicely.

Southern California

THE SALTON SEA

Southeast of Palm Springs, California is the 30-mile-long Salton Sea, a prime recreational ground for city-bound Southern Californians. Bombay Beach is only one of a variety of possible put-in points. At 235 feet below sea level this area is going to be mighty hot in summer; if you're traveling some distance to the area in a car without air-conditioning, you and your family will be in for some severe overheating. On our own trip, we passed Needles, California at 9 p.m. and the temperature was 114 degrees. Think about springing for air conditioning.

This area is a powerboat paradise, and a small sailboat can find itself wallowing in the wakes of an endless procession of motorboats—without the privacy offered by the nooks and crannies of Powell and Mead.

Relaxing on the Great Salt Lake's Antelope Island. Courtesy of the Utah Travel Council.

High Desert Lakes

THE GREAT SALT LAKE

This is one strange place. The salinity of the Great Salt lake is several times that of seawater. As the lake shrinks (as it's doing at this writing) strange salt-crystal formations spring up along the newly-exposed shoreline. (Give outboards a good flushing out in fresh water after running in this stuff.) The salt water is especially buoyant; you'll float so high you can read a newspaper while you're in the water—at least you can if you're middle-aged. This location will have a distinctly different feel from either Powell or Mead. You won't be enclosed by the scenery in the same way; the elevated surroundings are off in the distance here. You also have the metropolitan setting of Salt Lake City nearby, with its amenities and points of interest.

LAKE TAHOE

Lake Tahoe, split by the California-Nevada border, has the snowcapped peaks of the Sierra Nevadas on its horizon. Like Salt Lake, it's surrounded by very dry land. Like Salt Lake, it's not bounded by high cliffs cut by deep canyons. You're likely to see more power than sail here, but there at least should be lots of elbow room; it's a big lake. A year-round resort, Tahoe has its own brand of nearby entertainments. As with some other mountain lakes near mining operations, Tahoe has higher-than-normal mercury levels; be cautious here, and elsewhere, when eating local fish.

PYRAMID LAKE

Here's another high desert lake that might interest you if you don't mind being away from the shoreside attractions—or if you prefer it that way. Pyramid lake is northeast of Tahoe in the Virginia Mountains of western Nevada. The towns of Sutcliffe and Pyramid have supplies, laundry, and amenities.

FLAMING GORGE LAKE

Flaming Gorge dam backs Wyoming's Green River into an impressive lake near the border corners of Utah, Wyoming, and Colorado. It resembles Lake Powell in that it's enclosed by spectacular high canyon walls. In this setting, winds can be unpredictable, but the scenery is so gratifying and so immediate you may not care. From Manila, on the southwest side of the lake, you've got some 40 miles of solitude to explore.

Flaming Gorge Dam backs up a 91-mile-long lake at capacity. Pressed by steep-walled, vividly hued cliffs and forested mountains, the lake is a tourist's paradise. Courtesy of the Utah Travel Council.

Getting Information: Desert States

Arizona Office of Tourism
1100 West Washington Street
Phoenix, AZ 85007
602-542-8687

Utah Travel Council
Council Hall
Capitol Hill
Salt Lake City, UT 84114
801-538-1030

Nevada Commission on Tourism
Capitol Complex
Carson City, NV 89710
702-687-4322

New Mexico Tourism and Travel Division
Joseph Montoya Building
1100 St. Francis Drive
Santa Fe, NM 87503
505-827-0291

California Office of Tourism
1-800-862-2543 Ext. A1002

CHAPTER 14

Rocky Mountain Lakes

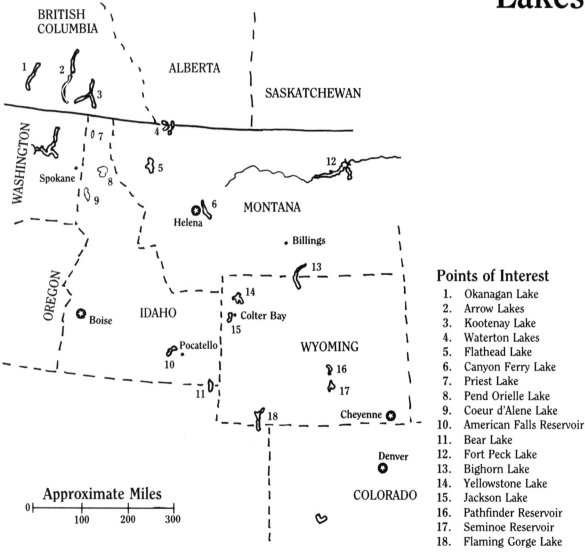

BRITISH
COLUMBIA

ALBERTA

SASKATCHEWAN

WASHINGTON

Spokane

OREGON

Boise

IDAHO

Helena

MONTANA

· Billings

Colter Bay

Pocatello

WYOMING

Cheyenne

Denver

COLORADO

Points of Interest

1. Okanagan Lake
2. Arrow Lakes
3. Kootenay Lake
4. Waterton Lakes
5. Flathead Lake
6. Canyon Ferry Lake
7. Priest Lake
8. Pend Orielle Lake
9. Coeur d'Alene Lake
10. American Falls Reservoir
11. Bear Lake
12. Fort Peck Lake
13. Bighorn Lake
14. Yellowstone Lake
15. Jackson Lake
16. Pathfinder Reservoir
17. Seminoe Reservoir
18. Flaming Gorge Lake

Approximate Miles

0   100   200   300

THIS IS THE region of North America I want to return to most badly. The scenery is breathtaking. There's Yoho National Park in the Canadian Rockies. "Yoho" was taken from the local Indian dialect, meaning "Yahoo!" or "O Boy!" or "Oh my God," or something like that. (If you ever wondered whether the Indians, born into this scenery, were as flabbergasted by it as tourists are, now you know. They appreciated it enough to live in it year round.)

The Rocky Mountain system is so vast that its north-south axis runs the length of the whole continent. If you're planning a trip and want to see some of it, decide what *else* you want to see, then pick a slice of the mountains that is most convenient to your trip. You'll head home knowing that there are many spectacular vistas you've missed. Personally, nothing moves my insides around quite as much as the sight of snow-capped mountains on the horizon. As you gather travel brochures, look for the views you like most and head for those. I'm not going to touch on the scores of smaller lakes scattered across this region. Understand that the smaller lakes have their own treasures. Some of them are too small to be much more than reflecting pools for the view; some are not intended for trailerable boats, and so no access roads or ramps are provided. Canoes and kayaks can be portaged in, though. Basically these lakes are suitable for a cautious **novice;** because of the frigid waters, a capsize could be dangerous.

There are so many lakes here that it makes sense to alter our organizational approach a little and review them state by state and province by province.

Colorado Lakes

While there is unbelievable scenery in Colorado, large lakes are not really part of it. Rocky Mountain National Park northwest of Denver is worth a look though; there are several large lakes within its borders, Lake Granby being the largest with a length of around 10 miles. If you're carrying a cartop boat or sailing canoe, the park could be a vacation in itself.

Wyoming Lakes

I've already mentioned Flaming Gorge Lake in the state's southwest corner, but it could as easily be included here. The 50-mile-long lake has its own national recreation area and would be on your Rocky Mountain driving route.

Jackson Lake is one of the most beautiful places in the state and a good choice for a visit. You're in the Grand Teton National Park (an awesome drive in and out) with park campgrounds at Lizard Creek and Snake River.

Yellowstone Lake in the national park is spectacular and is surrounded by other famous points of interest. The only problem with the place is its national repute: You can, during the peak tourist crunch, find yourself stacked bumper-to-bumper behind a long line of motor homes—

all of them intent on sampling the delights of a serene wilderness experience while hermetically sealed and untouched by the hand of Man. This spectacle is proper cause for laughter or tears—or both. The park is certainly one of our national treasures; maybe it would be best sampled in the off season, before or after the crunch. If you're headed that way, call the park service a day or so ahead and ask how crowded things are.

Remember to ignore the bears and to take care that they don't smell edibles in your car, boat, or tent that might remind them of the trash cans they've learned to rummage through. Bears have enormous upper-body development connected to claws like pruning hooks. Still, to put things in perspective, of the 698 fatalities in our national parks since 1984, only two have been caused by wild animals.

Montana Lakes

The mountain scenery can swallow you up and keep you moving happily from place to place for the duration of an average vacation. You'll have to decide whether you prefer the slow-paced rhythm of intricately exploring one place or the variety of a pogo stick approach, sampling first one place, then moving right along to another. If I could plan several seasons at once, I'd sample a region first pogo style, then return for a lingering stay in whatever turned out to be my favorite. Southeast of the state capital Helena you'll find Canyon Ferry Lake, created by the Canyon Ferry Dam on the Missouri River. The lake is some 25 miles long and nestled down in the Big Belt Mountains.

Hungry Horse Reservoir, a narrow but around 30-mile-long lake in northwest Montana, affords views of both the Swan and Flathead mountain ranges. You can find provisions and amenities at nearby Columbia Falls. The campsite at Murray Bay is your most practical starting point.

Most of the mountain lakes tend to be scenic but kind of skinny, nestled as they are between the long mountain ridges. Southwest of Hungry Horse, Flathead Lake offers more open space than any other lake in the region; it's some 30 miles long and some 10 miles across. Flathead Lake sits among a number of small towns and is surrounded by eight recreation areas or state parks; take your pick.

Here's a way to visit Canada by water. Lake Koocanusa is around 75 miles long, a third of it in British Columbia. Take advantage of Kootenai National Forest's campsites for a base camp and launch pad.

Sitting in southern Montana's Bighorn Mountains and extending south into Wyoming, Bighorn Lake is surrounded by a national recreation area. Its mountain vistas will be surpassed by locations farther north, but if you're an American history buff, there are other attractions. You're in Custer country; the monument at Little Bighorn is a relatively short drive from the lake.

WATERTON GLACIER INTERNATIONAL PEACE PARK

This place, part of Glacier National Park, is a visual feast and a chance to pogo from view to incredible view without driving any distance at all. The park straddles the US-Canadian border and encompasses eight lakes fed by the Waterton Glacier. (We had a rainy day in the mountains of Alberta,

Ice-blue water threading through snow-capped mountains: What can beat sailing in a place like this? Courtesy of Travel Montana.

so rather than hunker down in the cabin, we took off to see the Athabasca Glacier. You might do the same.)

Idaho Lakes

For most people in the country, Idaho calls to mind a vagueness . . . potatoes maybe. It's a mountain state rich in scenery. For example:

The American Falls Reservoir near Pocatello in the southeast corner of the state is not only a worthwhile stopping point on its own, but is a short hop from the Craters of the Moon National Monument. If you're traveling with family who are less enthusiastic about sailing than you are, it's a good and democratic strategy to select destinations where the boat is not the only path to their enjoyment. Something beautiful and weird like "moon craters"—actually lava formations—makes sense.

The 16-mile-long Priest Lake in the northern part of Idaho's panhandle is unusually beautiful—even by the standards of this region. Coolin on the lake's south shore would make a good provisioning point.

Still in mountainous western Idaho, but a bit farther south, is Coeur d'Alene Lake, another beautiful spot. The lake zigs and zags more than 20 miles, nestled in mountain scenery. Chatcolet on the south shore is a good place to start.

Nearby and even larger is the 35-mile-long Pend Oreille Lake. The shoreside towns of Hope, East Hope, Bayview, Lakeview, and Glengary can provide ground support for vacation sailing.

British Columbia and Alberta Lakes

Drive northeast from Seattle or Vancouver, and you'll come upon the 30-mile-long, islanded Harrison Lake. Harrison Hot Springs is nearby; one of several such places in the Canadian Rockies. If you've never soaked

Buffeted by steady mountain breezes on an Idaho lake. Courtesy Andrew Rafkind.

out of doors in a steaming hot pool, surrounded by snowcapped peaks, you've missed out on an earthly delight.

Continuing northeast along the Trans-Canada highway, you come to Shuswap Lake, which is shaped like a wobbly "H." You can sail at least 35 miles from the bottom of one corner to the top of another. The mountains here were less snowcapped than the ones we found farther east. The lake is popular, with a number of civilized shorefront locations—Sorrento and Celista, to name two.

The 65-mile-long Kootenay Lake lies north of the Idaho border to the southeast of Shuswap. If your family prefers to enjoy its scenery without being completely out of touch with civilization, this is an interesting choice, as there are enough settled locations surrounding the lake to offer amenities at the end of each day's sail—if you wanted to arrange things that way.

Okanagan Lake just south of Shuswap is near a major town (Kelowna) but it's otherwise less settled than Kootenay Lake. Okanagan Mountain Provincial Park is a logical starting point.

The Arrow Lake system covers some 100 miles. This is another relatively skinny mountain lake, running north-south through awesome scenery. Edgewood, Needles, Beaton, Shelter Bay, and Galena Bay, all are lakeside supports, as are a number of provincial parks, including Valhalla and Syringa Creek.

Kinbasket Lake (McNaughton Lake on old maps) at the foot of the Rockies near the Alberta border is another long lake, running almost 100 miles north. There are *no* towns along it anywhere, making it more of a wilderness experience to sail on it. We followed a sign that read "Big Lake Resort" down a steep dirt road to a campsite at the lake's edge. From this lake, you can see the 12,000-foot peak of Mt. Columbia. It's all spectacular, every way you look.

The last lake you pass on your route out of the Canadian Rockies to Calgary is Lake Minnewanka in western Alberta. It's small but surrounded by majestic peaks. Motorboats are permitted on the lake. (They are *not* permitted on some of the scenic lakes—a charming idea.)

Getting Information: Rocky Mountain Region

Wyoming Travel Commission
I-25 at College Drive
Cheyenne, WY 82002
307-777-7777

Idaho Department of Commerce
Travel Promotion
700 West State Street
Boise, ID 83720
208-334-2470

Travel Montana
Department of Commerce
Helena, MT 59620
406-444-2654

Colorado Tourism Board
1625 Broadway
Suite 1700
Denver, CO 80202
1-800-433-2656

Alberta Tourism
Box 2500
Edmonton
Alberta T5J 2Z4 CANADA
1-800-661-8888

CHAPTER **15**

California and Points South

Approximate Miles

0 —|——|——|——|——|
  100 200 300 400

1 Goose Lake area

2 □

Eureka 3 ○

4 ♗

5 ○

★ Sacramento

7 6

8 San Francisco

CALIFORNIA

• San Luis Obispo

9

Los Angeles

10 13

12 11 • San Diego

Tijuana 14 15

Ensenada 16 • Nogales

MEXICO

17

18

Gulf of Mexico

20

21

Pacific Ocean

Mulege •

19

La Paz

Cabo San Lucas

Mazatlan

Gulf of California

Points of Interest

1. Goose Lake
2. Shasta Lake
3. Lake Almanor
4. Lake Oroville
5. Clear Lake
6. Mono Lake
7. San Francisco Bay
8. Monterey Bay
9. Morro Bay
10. Channel Islands
11. Santa Catalina Islands
12. San Clemente Island
13. Salton Sea
14. Mouth of the Colorado
15. Bahia de Adair
16. Bahia de San Jorge
17. Bahia Kino
18. Isla Tiburon
19. Bahia Santa Maria
20. Laguna Madre
21. Laguna de Tamaihua

CALIFORNIA IS LIKE a country in itself, with snowcapped mountains, deserts, temperate forests with immense trees as old as history, and spectacular seacoasts. In addition, the works of civilization are here in abundance too; there is something for everyone. South of the border, Mexico offers both sumptuous tourist spas and places you can sail in absolute solitude. North Americans are fond of joking about Mexican inconveniences, but in actuality the Mexican government takes tourism very seriously. Reduced oil revenues place a new value on tourist income. Leave your preconceptions at home and see for yourself.

Lakes of California

Let's start at the Oregon border and head south. The inland corridor of California is an almost continuous band of state and national forests, including the famous Yosemite National Park, which are dotted with wilderness lakes. Near the town of Dorris is Lower Klamath Lake and National Wildlife Refuge. You're near Lava Beds National Monument, a strange place; it's also in the Klamath National Forest. Farther east are Tule Lake and Clear Lake Reservoir. The largest of these border lakes is Goose Lake, well over 20 miles long. The town of New Pine Creek is nearby; to the west is Modoc National Forest.

Driving south through the center of the state you'll have the snow-capped 14,000-foot Mount Shasta on the horizon. The Whiskeytown-Shasta-Trinity National Recreation Area holds two big lakes with up to 20-mile stretches affording a view of Mount Shasta. Clair Engle Lake is the westernmost of the two, near the town of Trinity Center. Shasta Lake is farther east with O'Brien and Lakehead for shoreside supports. Still farther east, on the western border of the Lassen National Forest, is slightly smaller Eagle Lake. This is beautiful country, and if you've just come from the desert states, you'll appreciate the relief from the heat.

At the southern end of the Mendocino National Forest, you'll find the sizable Clear Lake near the towns of Lakeport and Nice.

Moving east and slightly north from there you'll find Lake Oroville spreading its long and delicate fingers into the Plumas National Forest.

A floating marina on Shasta Lake in northern California.

The lake is part of a state recreation area that bears its name. Farther northeast is a somewhat smaller lake in an interesting setting. Lake Almanor sits near Lassen Peak in the Lassen National Forest and the Lassen Volcanic National Park. You're near the town of Wonderful, which about sums up local feelings about this place.

Southeast of Lake Tahoe is Mono Lake, which has several islands near the center. It's a state recreation area, just west of Yosemite National Park, which is worth a look if you can bear to share the view with so many of your countrymen. It's hard to think of a view as a product, but maybe it's come to that.

In the Sequoia National Forest, farther south, is Lake Isabella. Don't pass through this area without beholding these magnificent trees, the largest of which began to grow well before the Middle Ages. Wofford Heights and Weldon are nearby, as is Miracle Hot Springs.

All the lakes mentioned can be explored comfortably by **novice** sailors. The swimming is more comfortable than in many of the Rocky Mountain Lakes, adding to their appeal.

Bays of California

The northern California coast is a bold, spectacular shoreline with relatively few points of refuge. The northernmost shelter is Humboldt Bay, which is protected by a barrier peninsula near Eureka and Fields Landing in redwood country. This is not a huge area to sail in, but it might make an interesting layover and base camp while you look around. Fort Humboldt State Historical Park is here.

Just north of San Francisco is Tomales Bay State Park and the Point Reyes National Seashore. A finger of the Pacific curls almost 20 miles behind a scenic peninsula. Dillon Beach, Marshall, and Inverness provide shoreside support. Local piloting knowledge for both these little bays—currents and sea conditions—is important to have before attempting to tiptoe back out into the Pacific. In general, slack tide is best to come in or out of any such place.

Farther south is one of the jewels of the Pacific coast—San Francisco Bay. While winds are mild here in the winter, the wind machine really cranks here in the summer, blowing close to gale force many afternoons. You'll need a boat set up for rigorous sailing: reef points on your mainsail are a must, as is a good motor to help you along if things get too intense. (Jib and outboard can be an effective combination, the motor helping you point up, the jib adding needed drive. You can tack to windward this way with reasonable security if you have to.) The spectacular Golden Gate Bridge, Alcatraz Island, and Angel Island State Park, not to mention the San Francisco skyline are all enticements to set out and brave the winds. If you've got young children or anyone who isn't up for it, think twice before setting out. This isn't for the fainthearted or the novice. Candlestick Park State Recreation Area can provide a helpful ground support. As there aren't many good anchorages out there, most people daysail.

To the north, San Francisco Bay becomes San Pablo Bay, with China Camp State Park on the San Rafael peninsula nearby. The winds here will be lighter in the morning and tend to build up to full strength by

A Molly catboat barrels along in the typically strong winds of San Francisco Bay. Courtesy of Molly Catboats.

afternoon. Watch for fog, which can blow in on the prevailing westerly at any time. Just past Benicia you'll find Suisun Bay. The Sacramento and San Joaquin rivers empty into the bay, forming an intricate maze of waterways called the "California Delta." The water should be warmer in here than the near frigid waters of the bay. San Francisco Bay and its extensions offer a multitude of sailing grounds—all within reach of a city with unusual charms.

Farther down the coast is a city that got me wondering if I might not want to live there: Monterey. Despite the touristy embellishments, the town has enough of its old waterfront charm left to seem comfortable—especially taken in from the cockpit of a small boat. The harbor opens easily into the Pacific. On a good day, you could sample the big swells and snoop around. You're near Carmel, too, and all its spectacular vistas.

If you're taking the Pacific Coast Highway, you'll feel more secure if you're headed north with your car and trailer on the *inside* edge of the roadway than going south with your rig on the outside edge of the most scenic oblivion imaginable.

The Los Angeles area is huge and its industrial seaport isn't the place for fun. There are three yachting centers near Los Angeles that offer pleasant alternatives. From any of these locations, you can drive to Universal Studios, Disneyland, and the countless other area attractions. For children, for whom a steady diet of sailing is too much of the same thing, this area could be particularly attractive.

Marina del Rey is the northernmost choice. Parking and ramps for trailerable boats are extensive; hundreds of trailerable boats bake in the sun behind a storm fence, awaiting their owners' interest. The actual marina is an unbelievable immensity of wall-to-wall yachts. It boggles the mind to see so many lying in idle row after row. It reminded me of a colorful civilian version of the U.S. Navy's "mothball fleet" in Philadelphia. Given the numbers of pleasure boats there, the investment may

Wall-to-wall boats in Marina del Rey, California.

even be comparable. *Fearless* was dwarfed by most of the yachts in the harbor, but at least her sail was up.

Long Beach Marina to the south of L.A. is the next possible haven for a yachtsman. If a Navy man I met speaks truly, this harbor has been the starting point for several little Potters who eventually ended up in Hilo, Hawaii. It's a cheap but punishing way to get there.

Newport Bay is the southernmost of L.A.'s major marinas. Here, you have some 17 miles of waterway to explore. You'll see some beautiful boats parked in front of impressive real estate. Newport Beach is a popular swimming and surfing spot.

Just north of San Diego is Mission Bay. It's hardly rural, but there are islands and channels to explore, and you can visit Sea World while you're at it.

Finally you've made it all the way south to San Diego Bay. The mild climate and the 14 miles of waterways make this a major yachting center and a springboard for larger yachts heading off to Mexico or for places far more distant.

Sailing the California Coast

Because of the distance between sheltered areas, usually 50 miles at least, and because of the rugged nature of the shoreline, this is not an ideal area to do coastal sailing in a small boat. If your boat and your experience are up to an offshore sail, you can venture out from Long Beach or Newport Beach and sail the 26 miles to Santa Catalina Island or continue still farther out to San Clemente Island. Remember that in a small boat 26 miles is divided by your hull speed in whatever winds you've got. Going out, you'll most likely be beating to windward. Start out very early in the morning to avoid having to make your landfall in the dark. Bring a good compass, charts, and some experience at this sort of thing. On your return, you should make better time. Check the weather before starting out and back.

Lost? Look for planes returning from the Orient to the Los Angeles International airport. Contrails point the way. Ferries traverse the 26 miles from Long Beach and Newport; look for those too. If you have a cheap transistor radio aboard, you can use it as a crude radio direction finder. Point the antenna parallel to the horizon and aim it at the coastline. When it points *directly* at the radio station that's being received, you'll lose the signal. Since disc jockeys routinely mention their home city, you can get a bearing on the tower. Switch stations and take another bearing. Where the bearing lines cross, you've fixed your position—sort of.

There are other islands farther north: Santa Cruz, Santa Rosa, and San Miguel in the Santa Barbara channel, and not close to any harbor or shelter. For this, and because of the prevailing winds and frequent fog, even larger yachts pass these by in favor of Santa Catalina and San Clemente. I don't recommend these to small boat sailors unless the act of accomplishing the passage is its main reward and you have the boat, experience, and crew to give you some margin of safety.

Sailing in Mexico

The sailing opportunities of North America do not end at the Mexican border. For years, mariners have been sailing south along the Pacific coast of Mexico's Baja Peninsula, then rounding up into the Gulf of California. The trip along the Pacific coast has long been considered an arduous one, although now the government of Mexico is constructing an archipelago of marinas, each about a day's sail from the next. Still, these are average distances for yachts two or three times the size of the boats we're trailering. You can get to the Gulf of California more rapidly by car—to the spots too far north to interest the yacht that must round the tip of the Baja and sail all the way up.

Why go to the Baja? First of all, because it's beautiful. There is something unearthly about the combination of blue water against the beige, sunwashed sandstone. There are fantastic rock formations and a multitude of coves and corners in this landscape formed by the seismic wrenching away of the land here long ago. There is both the allure of privacy in the unexploited vastness of this area and the interesting possibility that the people you do meet may not be identical to you.

Depending on where in the Gulf of California you're headed, you can enter Mexico at Mexicali or at Tijuana, or, if you're headed for points farther down on the mainland side, you may enter at Nogales, just south of Tucson, Arizona. You can obtain tourist cards at the border; no visas are required. You will need proof of your American or Canadian citizenship, though. You will also need to obtain permits for your car, boat, and trailer. Mexico will not recognize the validity of your automobile insurance; you'll need to take out a short-term policy at the border. For a free book, *Know Before You Go,* write U.S. Customs Service, Washington, D.C. 20229.

We'll assume, for the areas covered in this book, that the road surfaces will be adequate for your family car. Mexican gasoline is often 65 octane—lower than our economy brands. A Costa Rican gentleman told me that his countrymen routinely bring mothballs (pure naphtha, he said) and drop in four of them with every 10 gallons of gas to improve the car's performance. I'm offering this Latin improvisation for your consideration. It has a certain elegance.

The Colorado River empties into the Gulf of California at its northern extremity at a place called the Golfo de Santa Clara. The area is close to the border and would be an interesting place to explore in a shoal draft boat. Let's proceed down the mainland coast first. A good friend has praised Puerto Peñasco at the Bahia de Adair for its friendly, uncommercialized charm. If you continue down the mainland coast, you can launch at Bahia de San Jorge and sail behind the protection of a long barrier island. All but one of the gulf's islands are uninhabited. The Bahia Kino is yet another point of interest, with the large Isla Tiburon offshore. You'll have covered around 300 miles by the time you get to the coastal town of Guaymas. From there it's a long hot drive to the town of Los Mochis. Go south to Pericos, the closest town to the Bahia Santa Maria and Isla Altamura. Some of Mexico's spectacular resort cities are much farther south along this coast, but you can get the full flavor of the Gulf of California within this stretch of coast. If Mazatlán and the other resorts appeal, and they may, consider flying in and renting a small sailboat once you're there. Leave the kids at home and make it a romantic occasion to feed your marriage.

If you choose to follow the Baja's eastern coast, the seaport San Felipe is about 120 miles south of the border. Halfway down the peninsula, a good trek, is the seaport of Santa Rosalia, which is connected by ferry to Guaymas across the gulf. About 700 miles down the coast is Loreto, a sprouting town that's going to be quite a spot, with its own airport. Whether it can simultaneously hang on to its old charm remains to be seen. Since old-fashioned charm does not, in and of itself, feed local children, one cannot blame seacoast communities for wanting to exploit their scenic resources to the fullest. And the scenic resources here are significant.

You can sail among islands offshore too. By the time you get to Bahia La Paz, you'll have covered 1,000 miles of the Baja. The city of La Paz sits in the cusp of a big, natural bay. It's a favorite spot for sailors rounding into the Gulf of California from the Pacific. A ferry runs from here across the gulf to the mainland attractions of Los Mochis and Mazatlan.

From Cabo San Lucas at the Baja's tip, you can get a ferry all the way to Puerto Vallarta near Guadalajara. Time and money permitting, you can see quite a bit of this region without having to sail any more of it than you want to.

MEXICO'S GULF COAST

You'll enter Mexico at Matamoros, just south of Brownsville, Texas. Mexico's Laguna Madre covers some 120 miles of coastline. From Matamoros it's around 350 miles to the Laguna de Tamiahua, near Tampico, an impressive bay behind a barrier island.

There are many reasons to visit Mexico, the historical wonders left by the Mayan civilizations among them. Realistic coverage of trailer sailing Central America would be a book in itself.

Getting Information: California and Points South

National Park Service
Western Regional Office
GGNRA
Fort Mason, Building 201
San Francisco, CA 94123
415-556-0560

California Office of Tourism
800-862-2543 Ext. A1002

Mexican Tourist Council
405 Park Avenue, Suite 1002
New York, NY 10022
212-755-7261
or
Secretariat of the State of Tourism
Avda Presidente Masaryk 172, 3xx
11587 Mexico, DF

CHAPTER 16

The Pacific Northwest

Points of Interest

1. Cape Scott
2. Queen Charlotte Strait
3. Port Hardy
4. Strait of Georgia
5. Knight Inlet
6. Glendale Cove
7. Campbell River
8. Jervis Inlet
9. Harrison Hot Springs
10. Fraser River
11. Arrow Lakes
12. Kootenay Lake
13. Franklin D. Roosevelt Lake
14. Grand Coulee Dam
15. San Juan Islands
16. Juan de Fuca Strait
17. Pacific Rim National Park
18. Puget Sound
19. Dabob Bay
20. Leadbetter State Park
21. Loomis Lake State Park
22. Columbia Bar
23. Reedsport
24. Coos Bay
25. Brookings Harbor
26. Deschutes National Forest and Lakes
27. Malheur Lake
28. Summer Lake
29. Lake Albert
30. Upper Klamath Lake
31. Goose Lake
32. Prince William Sound
33. Cook Inlet
34. Cross Sound
35. Tongass National Forest

IF THE ROCKY Mountains contain the most beautiful freshwater scenery on the continent, then the Pacific Northwest contains the most beautiful saltwater scenery anywhere in the world. Much of the coastline is remote, some of it unreachable by highway. While a larger cruising boat can make its way along great distances of coastline, such a cruise is an undertaking for an **expert** or an **adventurer** who is seeking not only relative solitude but a higher element of risk than most trailer sailors with families would wish to take. There are a number of places where any competent sailor *can* enjoy this magnificent area with no unusual element of risk. It will be these areas that get our primary focus.

There are some interesting lakes in this region, but the area's unique charms are its saltwater opportunities. Bear in mind that while a warm-water ocean current bathes much of the East Coast, a *cold*-water current washes much of our west coast. Dress for cooler weather and take extra precautions against capsize. If you're fleeing a hot, muggy summer, this region might be a dream come true on the basis of climate alone. Much that is true about the Maine coast will be true about this coast also: You'll be dealing with strong tides, strong currents, occasional fog, and rocky shores. In addition, a number of refuges along the Pacific coast have sand bars at their mouths that can become impassible in stormy weather. A boat in bad conditions must either stand out to sea to avoid being blown onto shore, or attempt to seek shelter in the lee of a point or an island and ride uneasily at anchor until conditions improve. These are not conditions for which small craft are suited, so while small boat passages through the Strait of Juan de Fuca, the Strait of Georgia, and up Queen Charlotte Strait have been made successfully, they are far from typical of what I would suggest. I've been sailing all my life, but I do not feel qualified to take on the outer Pacific Northwest coast, though there are spots inside Vancouver Island that I'd look forward to sampling.

Rivers of the Pacific Northwest

The Columbia River, which forms part of the Washington-Oregon border, offers the best sailing opportunities for small craft. The Columbia runs far into the interior and drops spectacular distances on its route to the sea. The river opens up near its mouth for roomy small boat sailing in beautiful countryside. While there are some large ocean-going yachts that put out to sea from Astoria, Oregon, the Columbia Bar at the mouth of the river is one of the most dangerous spots for small craft imaginable. Even Coast Guard lifesaving vessels have been overwhelmed at the mouth of the Columbia by mountainous seas breaking over the bar. If you're traveling a long distance to this region, there are far safer places to explore than the Columbia River as it meets the Pacific. The river is navigable by small boats along much of its length, with marinas and ramps inland in Portland and well upriver. Sections of the river are hotbeds of sailboarding. Here's a thought for the stouthearted: get a waterproof backpack and a wet suit and explore some of the area's waterways by boardboat!

Lakes of the Pacific Northwest

An upper stretch of the Columbia River in north-central Washington is blocked by the Grand Coulee Dam, producing an enormous amount of hydroelectricity and the roughly 200-mile-long Franklin Roosevelt Lake. If you're crossing the northern part of the U.S. en route to the Pacific Northwest, make this lake a stopover. The Coulee Dam National Recreation Area is lakeside. Pay the dam a visit.

The Mount Hood, Deschutes, and Willamette National Forests create a mid-state strip of greenery in Oregon from the Washington border almost to California. The forests are sprinkled with lakes, turning the whole area into an ideal place for small-boat camping and exploring in mountainous pine forest.

In southern Oregon, four good-sized lakes beckon: Upper Klamath Lake near Klamath Falls, Summer Lake and Lake Albert near the town of Paisley, and Malheur Lake in Malheur National Wildlife Refuge. If the mountains are not as high as the Canadian Rockies they are just as beautiful. Few areas can combine such ocean charms and such inland assets. Klamath Lake alone is easily big enough to absorb a small sailboat for a week.

Bays, Sounds, and Straits of the Pacific Northwest

The generally magnificent Oregon coast has some harbors but no large bays comparable to those farther north. Coos Bay, about a quarter of the way up from the California border, is worth a visit. Stop there and visit the Oregon Dunes National Recreation Area. In Oregon the air, by midafternoon, often becomes incandescent; fantastic rock formations adorn the beaches. The Oregon Dunes seem to be transplanted from the Sahara, except that the air is temperate. The dunes are huge—well worth a detour if the area isn't a primary target.

Lost Lake isn't lost to Mt. Hood, which keeps watch from Oregon's Cascades. Courtesy of the Oregon Division of Travel.

Winchester Bay at Reedsport, Tillamook Bay between Tillamook and Garibaldi, and Nehalem Bay at Nehelam are all smaller bays but given the scenic appeal of the area, you might want to follow the coast, putting in for a seaside look as the spirit moves you. All these bays have ramp access, usually some distance up the rivers and creeks that flow into them.

Up the coast into Washington, and past the Columbia River, Willapa Bay hooks inland and south to form an interesting small-boat stopover. The bay is surrounded by state parks as well as the Willapa National Wildlife Refuge.

Another coastal harbor with sufficient room to interest a small-boat sailor is Grays Harbor, Washington, near Aberdeen and Ocean City State Park. There are dozens of state parks all along this magnificent coastline; campsites are plentiful along the coastal highway.

Remember that coastal harbors may not be safe to leave or enter under the wrong tidal or sea conditions; get local advice before setting sail. Do not risk an outboard failure on a windless day and see yourself swept out to sea over the bar.

The Strait of Juan de Fuca separating Washington from British Columbia leads you into some of the most spectacular sailing grounds in the world. Seattle, Tacoma, and Olympia, Washington look out over a small-boat paradise. Puget Sound is filled with a maze of islands from north of Seattle to Tacoma and beyond, all the way southwest to Olympia. Facilities abound. On the western side of Puget Sound is the Olympic National Forest; sail south through Dabob Bay past the towns of Quilcene and Brinnon, to Scenic Beach State Park.

Head to the top of Puget Sound and explore Oak Harbor, to the east of Whidbey Island. Sail Skagit Bay and Saratoga Passage past Everett; the Puget Sound area can absorb a decade of summers. You can sample views of rugged mountains within sight of saltwater coves, and while you have to mind the tides and the weather, you're sailing in protected water ideal for small boats.

If you sail north out of Puget Sound, you'll head into the San Juan Islands. You can get to the islands by ferry from Anacortes. The ferry takes you on a spectacular ride to Lopez Island, or you can stay on and reach other islands farther out. Lopez Island has a launch ramp, but at low tide both the dock and the ramp are completely dried out and surrounded by a broad rim of mud. You'll have to mind the tides, which drive a complex system of currents and eddies that swirls around the island. Knowledgeable locals can ride these, getting a boost from place to place. When we sailed among the islands, the breezes were very light and we depended on our outboard. A purist, traveling on sail and oars alone, could have a tedious time of it. This is a lovely area with gracious people. Visit Friday Harbor; if you're lucky, you'll see a few so-called killer whales.

Northwest of the San Juans is Vancouver Island and the lovely British Columbian capital city of Victoria. The Strait of Juan de Fuca, however, is a body of water to be taken seriously. Tides from both the Strait of Georgia and Puget Sound pour through Juan de Fuca, creating a huge and powerful volume of water. When the wind runs contrary to the

Beautiful bluewater cruising boats grace a harbor in the San Juans. The boat on the right sported a bright orange hull.

current—especially when the whole business collides with big Pacific swells, conditions that are very dangerous to small craft develop.

The Strait of Georgia runs for more than 130 miles north from Puget Sound and the Strait of Juan de Fuca narrowing as it passes through a maze of islands. Seafaring Indian tribes developed a culture that parallels that of the Vikings in some respects: Their love of adventure and violence, their skill in relatively small boats, their gift for artistry in wood. Abandoned villages and totem poles appear along the fog-shrouded coastline like phantoms from the past. The convoluted coastline offers countless refuges from foul weather and isolated places to explore—all within sight of rugged mountains inshore. Watch out for "deadheads"—waterlogged remnants of logging operations—often whole trunks—that lurk beneath the surface. Ramming one can hole your boat or trash your outboard.

North of Vancouver you'll find a number of bays cut deep into the shoreline: Horseshoe Bay with Cypress and Porteau Cove Provincial

Parks, and farther north, Saltery Bay. You can use the town of Egmont for shore support or camp at Saltery Bay Provincial Park, or Skookumchuck Narrows Provincial Park. If you want to do a bit of coastal sailing, you can sail to the northern end of the Strait of Georgia to Desolation Sound Marine Park. Follow the deep Toba Inlet almost 40 miles inland; it's incredibly beautiful. The water tends to warm up as you get farther north, making swimming a reasonable proposition.

From there you'd be doing a serious coastal navigating job in a small boat—and you'd *have to* because you could no longer trailer your boat along the coastline to any destination you want. Many northern seaport villages depend on water transport or seaplane for everything. Check regional maps to see if you can drive to areas that interest you.

It's about 1,500 miles from Vancouver to Juneau, Alaska—a long way to haul a boat. The immense distances are at once Alaska's boon and curse. The Far North remains the last refuge, not only of endangered wildlife, but of America's free spirits. If you can make it to Juneau, you can sail amid the island cluster of Admiralty Island National Monument. Northwest of Juneau the Taku Glacier lumbers into Cross Sound at the base of Fairweather Mountain. Just across the border in British Columbia, the peaks of the Alsek Range soar over 15,000 feet. You can base out of Juneau or camp in the Tongass National Forest. There is a ramp at nearby Haines as well as ample campsites.

From the town of Whittier southeast of Anchorage you can sail in beautiful Prince William Sound and explore its many islands (many of which will eventually free themselves from Exxon's 1989 generosity). Call the National Forest Service before setting out to see if and where you can launch.

There are boat ramps at Ketchikan, Craig, Wrangell, Petersburg, Sitka, Pelican, several in Juneau, Haines, and Yakutat along the southern Alaska coast. Some of these are seaplane ramps. In general, roads and basic conditions suggest a *very* portable boat on a beefed-up trailer, pulled by a husky vehicle in the prime of its life.

A ghostly herd of boats motors quietly into the mouth of British Columbia's Desolation Sound. Courtesy of the British Columbia Travel Division.

Finally, west of Anchorage, try camping at Lake Clark National Park & Preserve or Katmai National Park & Preserve and explore Kamishak Bay. You can explore Cook Inlet well inland—nearly 200 miles. Parts of this waterway may be less protected than the first two mentioned, though.

If you've got the time, a dependable car or truck, a solid trailer, and gas money, there's no reason why you can't take a stab at Alaska. If you can't go all the way, there's a wealth of incredible places to sail on the long road north.

Sailing the Pacific Northwest Coast

Sailing up the coast from Oregon to Vancouver Island in a small boat is not a prospect I would care to encourage here. An inland passage up the Strait of Georgia and Queen Charlotte Strait to the northern tip of Vancouver Island would be a challenging trip set off by spectacular scenery. I would sail in Puget Sound and maybe try out a trip to Desolation Sound before committing to anything so ambitious. On the east side of Vancouver Island you'll have Campbell River, Sayward, Alert Bay, and Port Hardy along your route. Mostly, you'll be on your own. That would be the chief appeal—and the chief peril—of such a trip. If you could do it safely, it would be an experience you'd remember the rest of your life. But then sailing almost *anywhere* in this region would be like that.

Getting Information: Pacific Northwest

National Park Service
Pacific Northwest Regional Office
83 South King Street
Suite 212
Seattle, WA 98104
206-442-5565

Alaska Public Land Information Center
605 West 4th Avenue
Anchorage, AK 99501
907-271-2737

Alaska Division of Tourism
PO Box E
Juneau, AK 99811
907-465-2010

Washington State Tourism Division
101 General Administration Building
11th and Columbia Streets
Olympia, WA 98504
206-753-5600

Oregon Economic Development Office
Tourism Department
595 Cottage Street Northeast
Salem, OR 97310
503-373-1270

British Columbia Ministry of Tourism, Recreation, and Culture
117 Wharf Street
Victoria
British Columbia Z8W 2Z2
CANADA
604-683-2000

CHAPTER **17**

The Canadian Subarctic

Points of Interest

1. Beaufort Sea
2. Aishihik Lake
3. Kluane Lake
4. Teslin Lake
5. Frances Lake
6. Williston Lake

7. Great Bear Lake
8. Mackenzie River
9. Great Slave Lake
10. Lake Claire
11. Lake Athabasca
12. Reindeer Lake
13. Frobisher Lake

14. Churchill Lake
15. Lesser Slave Lake
16. James Bay
17. Akimiski Island

Here you can choose to lose yourself totally in a vast wilderness unspoiled by the intrusive hand of man. This is *not* going to be like the other places mentioned in this book. You're heading back in time to settings where modern conveniences and population densities no longer apply; you'll have to absorb the implications, which are many.

Arctic Considerations

TRAVEL

Distances are long and roads are, as you go farther north, unpaved. Driving hundreds of miles on gravel roads may age your family car unmercifully. Consider putting snow tires on all four wheels to better resist punctures. Consider adding heavy-duty suspension and an extra undercoating to your vehicle. Gas stations are few and far between; how can you carry extra gas cans so they won't fly off? You will need spare tires and a supply of spare parts, fan belts etc. You might consider a heavy-duty oil cooling radiator and some extra cans of oil, oil filters, and air filters. The territories require that you drive with your lights on. You can purchase plastic light protectors locally. Bring an extra headlamp.

The extent of your precautions are directly dependent upon your interest in traveling beyond the range of paved highway systems. Four-wheel drive vehicles are ideal for off-road trips and for launching and retrieving boats from poorly-prepared ramps, or from beaches with no ramps at all. If you have a keen interest in really outbacking it, consider buying a vehicle designed for off-road use.

YOUR BOAT AND TRAILER

Sadly, most manufacturers of small boats put the least expensive trailers under them. Most customers have little real interest in the trailers under their boats. They want the lowest possible cost, usually. Since manufacturers usually take a mark-up on trailers, they also tend to look for

The rigors of travel suggest light trailerable boats or, better yet, car-toppers, for the Canadian subarctic. Courtesy Yukon Tourism.

minimal initial cost. If you intend to trailer your boat in rugged terrain, see if your boat is close to the trailer's maximum rated capacity. If so, you'll need to either replace it with a heavier-duty trailer or beef up the one you've already got. Heavier-duty tires and springs will help. A tongue extender might help you launch from poorly prepared areas.

Check tightness of nuts and bolts constantly and bring spares of both these and of the internal parts of the latch and ball mechanism of the hitch itself. Bring at least one spare tire, one can of aerosol "flat fixer," and a hand pump.

Don't haul some leviathan boat unless you relish the sheer challenge of trailering it. A simple boat will greatly reduce your cares. Not only should all loose equipment be tied down, but it should be *padded* as well. Your boat's tie-down straps should also be run through clear plastic hose to reduce chafing against the hull. Anything that can bounce off or unscrew itself will do so, dumping rudders, outboard motors, oars, oarlocks, booms, or more onto the highway in your wake. Gear inside your cabin is subject to the same shocks and requires the same consideration.

You may be a *long* way from the nearest marine supply shop. Fittings should be strong enough to serve without fail. Bring along extra rope and parts, and a few basic tools. Should your hull be punctured, you'll need a good bilge pump and maybe a supply of cheap inflatable toys that can be blown up inside the cabin to restore the boat to a useful waterline.

MISCELLANY

You'll need good, warm sleeping gear and clothing you can put on in layers to get adequate comfort. If you're considering ambitious sailing, consider wetsuits to preserve body heat in the event of capsize. Both car and boat will need good bug screens, and in some areas, you might consider screened-in bonnets like the ones beekeepers wear. A dependable insecticide is a necessity. Bring along extra water jugs and solar showers for areas where such facilities are not available. Bring extra toilet paper too. A citizen's band radio might not be a bad idea; for emergencies use Channel 9.

If you prepare like survivalists, you can enjoy an unusual degree of independence and see parts of the continent few people ever will.

Sailing the North Country

An arm of the Hudson Bay, James Bay sits like a beaver's tail between Quebec and Ontario. The explorer Henry Hudson was cast adrift here by his men over a disagreement on whether to continue or return to the relative security of the North Atlantic. You're at the approximate latitude beyond which trees cannot grow. The air has a crisp cleanness to it that tells you you're in the far north. You can get as far north as Matagami, Quebec on surfaced highway, then the road turns to packed gravel for the rest of the route. The shoreline is fairly well cut with coves here and the towns of Fort Rupert, Eastman, and Chisasibi (Fort George) dot the bay's east shore. La Grande Rivière connects Chisasibi with a large inland lake, Lac Sakami. It's awesomely remote; you're on your own.

If you're interested in getting away from it all but keeping to paved highways, consider trailering to the northern extensions of Manitoba's Lake Winnipeg, Lake Winnipegosis, Cedar Lake, or Clearwater Provincial Park on Clearwater Lake. You're about 400 miles north of the U.S. border in wild country infrequently visited. You can sail quite a distance up here. The sun will hardly set at night, so you may want light-proof curtains when you want to sleep. From the town of Lynn Lake, it's a relatively short distance to Reindeer Lake, but you should phone the Royal Canadian Mounted Police or maybe the Canadian Auto Association to make sure the "winter road" is passable.

You have to head west to Alberta or British Columbia to get started on a route that can take you all the way inside the Arctic Circle. The world's largest shopping mall in Edmonton is the last vestige of ultra-modernity you'll be seeing as you head even farther north. Regular highway can take you to Lesser Slave Lake and its provincial park. This is a huge lake by most standards, though far bigger bodies of water await you farther north. You can continue on paved highway to Hay River on the southern shore of Great Slave Lake in the Northwest Territories. Although this body of water is larger than Lake Ontario, there aren't more than half a dozen boats that sail up here. This is a rockbound glacially-formed lake and the water is *very* cold. There may not be useful weather reports on your radio, so a barometer might be handy to warn you of deteriorating conditions. A paved road will take you east to Pine Point. From there, you're on packed gravel roads. You can continue east to Fort Resolution, where the lake begins to break up into a maze of island passages, or you can head northwest to Fort Providence, Rae, and Yellowknife—the territorial capital. There are ghost-town ruins along the shores of the lake with untended tombstones out back. A sensitive photographer could have a field day in a place like this.

From Fort Resolution, you can proceed down gravel road to Carlson Landing to follow a winter road to Lake Athabasca. I've run across no literature of anyone sailing there. It's an outside chance you could be the first. Before going to the trouble, check to make sure the winter road is passable. Often the "winter roads" are ice roads—frozen creek beds passable only in winter for obvious reasons.

For destinations still farther north, head west to British Columbia and north by paved road to Whitehorse, the Yukon capital. There are some interesting lakeside spots on your route that might be worth a stop. Teslin on Teslin Lake is a taste of a frontier time gone by, and a shoreside support for lake sailing. Carcross (once called Caribou Crossing) has a population of 350 souls. A huge sternwheeler is pulled up on the town's lakefront. It's easily the largest edifice there. Destruction Bay on Kluane Lake is another colorful spot and a possible jump-off spot for a little lake sailing. The place was blown apart by a violent storm in 1940—hence the name. Population: 48.

From Whitehorse north, you're on the Dempster Highway's packed gravel road headed for the Arctic Circle. Pay attention when a service station's billboard says, "Last chance for gas/water!" There's not much on the way to the end of the line at Inuvik, near Mackenzie Bay. You're above the Arctic Circle here; the sun never sets. If you've never seen the northern lights, this is your best chance. If you've never seen reindeer before, this is your chance. You're on a reindeer grazing park. The Mackenzie River, the Arctic Red River and the Mountain River join and flow into the bay here. The Mackenzie is navigated by barges all the way from Great Slave Lake, but you'd have to fly back for your car. There is no bus service. From the town of Arctic Red River, you could go upriver roughly 100 miles to Inuvik and disembark there. If the current sweeps you by the last vestiges of civilization, you're off to never-never land and an interesting extinction in the Beaufort Sea—unless you could round Richards Island to Tuktoyaktuk, a settlement to your east. There is no land passage back to Inuvik.

The terrain here is essentially tundra, a boggy soil that supports a fly and insect population not to be believed. Screens and bug repellent are a must. Screened bonnets are recommended. The land here has an austere beauty. Nature seems to have stripped down everything to a bare minimum. Why go? I should think only people who are challenged by projects like this will respond to the prospect—and those who do will experience the kind of rarified satisfaction known by circumnavigators and the crossers of oceans.

Perhaps no region we've covered requires such research on your part as this one. Should you wish to push all the way to Inuvik, call ahead to make sure that their boat rental facilities will permit you to launch there—or recover it, should you approach from downriver. Several parks have a stay limit of 14 days. If you need an extension, see *in advance* if you can obtain one.

Getting Information: Canadian Subarctic

Arctic Hotline: 1-800-661-0788

Tourism Industry Association of the Northwest Territories
Box 506
Yellowknife
Northwest Territories X1A 2N4
 CANADA

Travel Yukon
PO Box 2703
Whitehorse
Yukon Y1A 2C6 CANADA

A Final Wish

I hope, of course, that you'll go sailing America. And I hope something happens to you while you're doing it. It could happen anywhere really—in the desert, in the ocean someplace, or maybe in the mountains. For me, it happens most often at night.

It starts with a tiny sound that wakes you up, or maybe it's a pressure in your bladder that does it; you stretch, drifting between dreams and consciousness. Quite suddenly you're awake, and since you are, you decide to poke your head out the hatch and have a look around. Maybe it's a bit chilly and you shiver a little while you're sliding open the hatch, quietly so it won't wake anyone. A blue light floods in and you stand up for a better look. The full moon bathes everything in its cool light. The deck is cold and dripping. A faint mist rises off the water, giving distant objects a spectral hesitancy. The air is heavy and still, the water like a mirror. The moon has laid a platinum trail that a spirit could walk upon, but not a man. This, it occurs to you, is what God is doing with the world when no one is looking. You have poked your nose into Nature's business when you should have been asleep. The clammy deck is intended to discourage you from venturing any farther—so you rest your chin on your knuckles and just look.

This is when it happens to you—if it ever will—and I hope it does. It breaks your heart. You feel a sigh well up in you like the lost chord, and you crouch there in the companionway mesmerized by what you have seen. If you're *really* lucky, someone you love appears at your side and the two of you just look. If not, you turn away from the sight and love the people you're with with all your might.

The same love goes out into scenery you no longer need to see and, at the very moment your heart breaks, you are miraculously expanded to enormous size. Your soul pours like smoke through the trees on the mountain ridges far above your head—then, in an instant, you're snapped back inside your own skin. It's just like seeing a meteor: The whole thing is so easy to miss if you're looking in the wrong place.

When you crawl back into your bunk you feel a little weird, knowing that something too huge to verbalize and too tiny to comment on has just happened to you, and changed you for the better.

Thoughts, Tips, and Lists for Sailing America

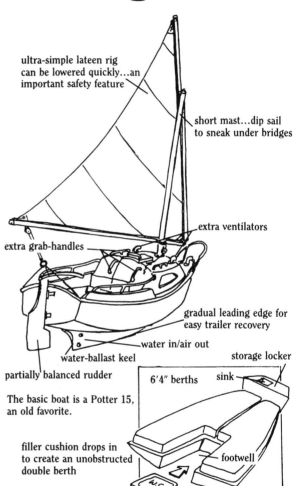

ultra-simple lateen rig can be lowered quickly...an important safety feature

short mast...dip sail to sneak under bridges

extra ventilators

extra grab-handles

gradual leading edge for easy trailer recovery

water in/air out

storage locker

partially balanced rudder

water-ballast keel

It looks as though we're going to start doing some more long-distance trailer sailing. Our Potter 19 has been easy for its size, but for really casual outbacking on lousy roads, nothing beats an ultra-light micro-cruiser. Here's my latest thinking: Every aspect of this design has been tested successfully. HMS Marine intends to offer the shoal-keel version as an option for longer-range sailors for whom the easiest launching and beaching characteristics of the standard boat are offset by the need for extra internal volume for storage. The sailing and safety qualities of the two approaches are about equal. The Potter sails nicely with a lateen rig and I've always preferred radical simplicity in my boats.

The basic boat is a Potter 15, an old favorite.

6'4" berths   sink

footwell

filler cushion drops in to create an unobstructed double berth

portable toilet slides out from under bridge deck

W.C.

Your Access to the Nation's Waterways

Something is going on around the United States that you should be aware of. It affects our access to the nation's waterways:

- The rise in real estate prices, especially in the value of waterfront property, is slowly squeezing marinas out of business. Condominiums and other land development schemes can wring far more profit out of water frontage than can marinas. Marinas must drastically raise rates for even common services or sell out—make their big one-time bundle—and find something else to do. Even while boating use is up, dockage is shrinking.
- Some of the new people living in their brand new waterfront properties are under the impression that they own the view to seaward. When a small boat drops the hook 50 yards off their beach, they reach for the phone to see if someone can be found to remove the blot from their seascape. They have, after all paid a bundle for the view; why should you enjoy it for free?
- The proliferation of boats on the nation's waterways is increasing demands for some form of regulation. The discourteous and unseamanlike behavior of some of these mariners lends some justification to these demands. Some communities are attempting to pass regulations against anchoring in community waters or imposing tariffs on out-of-towners for even entering their harbors. Several communities are being challenged in court at this writing.
- State governments, hard up for cash, look at "yachtsmen" as a population of fat-cats—and a useful source of revenue. User fees for ramps, parking, and land use are up, as are local taxes on boat ownership. Things may get more expensive.

It has been a long-standing tradition (and legal principle) that the national waterways are open corridors for public use. It is a violation of that tradition for communities to impose feudalistic taxes on passers-through. Also, we cannot permit a gradual gentrification of our waterways to deny citizens of average income access to the seas, bays, lakes, and gulfs. Democracy has always encouraged prosperity but been wary of privilege.

We can do something positive about these developments by joining BOAT/US (Boat Owners Association of the United States), 880 S. Pickett St., Alexandria, VA 22304. This is our national lobby in Washington. If we don't represent our interests, we'll live under the restrictions imposed on us by other interest groups more powerfully funded and represented.

Another national association is the National Association of State Boating Law Administrators (Small Craft Advisory), Box 19000, Seattle WA 98109.

Please write these organizations for information and support at least one of them.

The Drunken Sailor

In 1988 there were 946 boating fatalities in the U.S. The Coast Guard attributes more than half these deaths to operation while intoxicated. In song and folklore, sailors have had a reputation for (and a certain pride in) their prowess as two-fisted drinkers; we conveniently forget that back in the days of wooden ships and iron men, grog was tightly rationed at sea.

The launching ramp on the Arizona end of Lake Powell was by far the busiest put-in point I have ever seen. The boaters there were pretty typical of the norm, but it was informative to watch because there were so many of them in one place. I couldn't help noticing cases of beer and boxes bulging with hard stuff being loaded into boat after boat. No one would ever dream of setting off on the nation's freeways so fortified. Not even the most helpless alcoholic would take so much *specifically for the drive itself*—unless bent on murder or suicide.

How can I share with you all that I've learned while sailing America without sharing this?:

I've met many people whose dispositions are not improved by alcohol. Moreover, many men view their boat as an opportunity to enjoy an absolute authority denied them in any other setting. They are free to give vague, ambiguous orders. Sluggish or indecisive responses can provoke a rage worthy of Captain Bligh. What is exhilaration for the skipper can begin to feel like tyranny to the crew.

Alcohol mellows some people, hardens others. Anyone whose disposition is not sweetened by a drink or two should leave the stuff ashore and allow the natural tonic of the wind and water to work its magic, unimpeded by chemical interference.

The major objection I have to drinking at sea is that it compromises competence: the technical competence of drivers, surgeons, operators of machinery. It compromises the competence of people to be parents, children, husbands, wives, and friends. We drive much more often than we sail. When things go wrong on the water, or when something unexpected occurs, we can't draw on the instincts born of thousands of hours experience. We cannot be impaired. Alcohol gives us a surge of confidence when we least deserve to have one.

This book is an invitation to safety and enjoyment. In that vein I hope that sailors will wait till the day is done and, resting comfortably, lean back in the cockpit, break out the grog if they're so inclined, and watch the sun go down. That picture sounds awfully good to me. And it makes sense.

Trailering Safety Checklist

Whenever you stop for gas, food, or a rest, walk around the car and trailer and check the following:

- Trailer-to-car connection is solid
- Safety chains both hooked on
- Lights connected and working
- Boat tie-down straps secure

- Boat winched up tight onto trailer, handle tied down
- Lug nuts on wheels all tight
- Trailer hitch bolted tightly to car
- Good air pressure in tires

Vibration on the road is a continuous source of mischief. Your little trailer wheels spin much faster than your automobile tires. Things can come loose with amazing speed. To travel safely, you should have the following supplies in your car:

- A lug wrench that fits your trailer's wheels
- A crescent wrench
- Vise-Grip pliers
- A tire pressure gauge
- A spare trailer wheel and tire, inflated for use

Now you can go anywhere. Frequent checking is the key. Whenever you're in doubt about anything, pull over and check. You wouldn't want to lose your boat. Consider the carnage if your trailer disconnected and swerved into oncoming traffic.

Your Boat's Tool Kit

These are best kept in a small plastic tool or tackle box to prevent rust. We carry the following:

- A hand-powered drill and set of bits
- Needlenose pliers/wire cutters
- Vise-Grip pliers
- A wrench set
- A small assortment of nuts, bolts, washers, wood screws
- A Phillips and a slot-head screwdriver
- A roll of strong wire
- Needle and thread for sail repair
- A plug wrench for the outboard motor
- A spare spark plug

In a separate bag, we carry an assortment of lines tied in neat bundles plus a bunch of short sections for use as "stops" or tie-downs.

A Small First Aid Kit

Many pre-packaged first aid kits are available. We prefer to assemble our own, containing the following items:

- A box of Band-Aids
- Several larger bandages
- Adhesive tape
- An "ace" bandage with clips
- A bottle of Tylenol

- Antihistamines
- Antiseptic and lotion for cuts, scrapes, sunburn
- Some cotton swabs
- Scissors
- Insect repellent
- Bug bite lotion
- Sunscreen lotion and 100% sun block for nose, lips, etc.

For Safety

- Bring a Coast Guard-approved life preserver for each person on your boat.
- Tie whistles to each life preserver with a short cord.
- Clip a small waterproof light to each life preserver for night sailing.
- Have at least one throwable life cushion or ring.
- Carry an air horn for signaling.
- Install Coast Guard-approved running lights for use at night and carry a waterproof flashlight.
- Install solid grabrails on the cabin roof and wherever else hand-holds are needed. (Remember a child's reach is not as long as yours.)
- Tie a loop around one of the rudder gudgeons. Better yet, a permanently mounted boarding ladder provides a way to get back on board—especially for someone too young or too old to get back on board by brute force alone.
- Have a solid point of attachment for a lifeline or a safety harness in foul weather or at night.
- Carry a fire extinguisher.
- Carry Coast Guard-approved rescue flares.
- Keep an adequate anchor ready with at least 150 feet of strong line. Will your cleat or bow eye hold? Reinforce if needed.
- Have pump(s) with hose(s) long enough to reach into the cabin and to clear it of water.
- Carry a compass, always. Even a Boy Scout compass is better than nothing.
- Bring charts for your planned sailing waters.
- Leave a trip itinerary with a friend with instructions to call the Coast Guard if you don't phone in after a reasonable time.
- Check weather reports before setting out.
- Have first aid supplies aboard, always.

Things to Think of Before Departing

- Do you need special trip insurance? Does your boat's insurance cover the waters you plan to sail in *out of state?*
- Have you found a safe place for valuable stuff in the house?

- Have you stopped newspaper deliveries and asked a neighbor to pick up anything unexpected that shows up at your door?
- If you're going to be gone a long time, will someone mow the lawn and keep the place looking lived-in?
- Have you notified local police of your intention to be away so they can keep an eye out for you (if they can do that sort of thing)?
- Have you wired automatic timers to some of your lights so that the place seems occupied?
- Have you removed all smelly perishable foods from the icebox, turned off stove, iron, etc?
- If you're doing a long-distance sailing trip, have you filed a float plan with anyone (your route and expected times of arrival) so that the Coast Guard can take an educated guess where to look for you? (Remember to call in when you arrive safely.)

Useful Books and Videos

GENERAL SOURCES

Sailboat and Equipment Directory: published annually by *Sail* magazine, available at newsstands; 100 First Avenue, Charlestown, MA 02129.

Cruising World magazine: focus on world cruising, great fantasy stuff and practical tips; 5 John Clarke Road, Newport, RI 02840.

Small Boat Journal: has practical lore, boat reviews, and trip stories, ideal; 2100 Powers Ferry Road, Atlanta, GA 30339.

Sail magazine: more racing oriented, good how-to information, a solid general interest publication; 100 First Avenue, Charlestown, MA 02129.

ADDITIONAL SOURCES

International Marine Publishing Company: publishes and distributes a wide range of marine books and videos; Camden, ME; 800-822-8158.

Dolphin Book Club: distributes wide selection of marine publications; Camp Hill, PA 17012-0001.

The Armchair Sailor bookstore: offers a huge selection of mail order books; Lee's Wharf, Newport, RI 02840.

PRACTICAL INFORMATION

(A few of the following books are out of print; check used-book stores or libraries; the effort is worth it.)

Singlehanded Sailing, 2nd edition, by Richard Henderson. Camden, Maine: International Marine Publishing Company, 1988; a gold mine of useful information.

Sea Sense, 2nd edition, by Richard Henderson. Camden, Maine: International Marine Publishing Company, 1979 (out of print, 3rd edition will be published September, 1990); ditto.

Sailing on a Micro-Budget, by Larry Brown. Camden, Maine: Seven Seas Press, 1984; reviews approaches to small-boat cruising and types of boats and sail rigs.

Handbook of Trailer Sailing, by Robert Burgess. New York: Dodd, Mead & Company, 1984 (out of print); a wealth of tips for small-boat cruising.

100 Small Boat Rigs, by Philip C. Bolger. Camden, Maine: International Marine Publishing Company, 1986; lucid and educational with dry humor, a tinkerer's gold mine.

The Catamaran Book, by Brian Phipps. Hove, East Sussex, England: Fernhurst Books (distributed in the U.S. by International Marine Publishing Company), 1989; practical advice on all aspects of catamaran sailing.

Children Afloat, by Pippa Driscoll. Hove, East Sussex, England: Fernhurst Books, 1989 (distributed in the U.S. by International Marine Publishing Company), 1989; safety, organization, entertainment for children.

The Sailor's Sketchbook, by Bruce Bingham. Camden, Maine: Seven Seas Press, 1983; a zillion decorative and practical ideas to improve a boat, masterful artwork, too.

The Gourmet Galley, by Terence Janerico. Camden, Maine: International Marine Publishing Company, 1986; for fine cooking on small boats, more than 500 recipes . . . why eat canned stuff?

Upgrading Your Small Sailboat for Cruising, by Paul and Marya Butler. Camden, Maine: International Marine Publishing Company, 1988; title tells it all, specific nitty-gritty.

The Thousand Dollar Yacht, by Anthony Bailey. Camden, Maine: International Marine Publishing Company, 1988; wonderful insights and whimsical humor about cruising a home-built dory.

The Handbook of Sailing, by Bob Bond. New York: Alfred A. Knopf, Inc., 1980; I think this is the best learn-to-sail book around, lucidly and thoroughly illustrated.

A Cruising Guide to Narragansett Bay, by Lynda and Patrick Childress. Camden, Maine: International Marine Publishing Company, 1990; everything you wanted to know about sailing Narragansett Bay, and more.

A Cruising Guide to the Maine Coast, by Hank and Jan Taft. Camden, Maine: International Marine Publishing Company, 1988; the definitive guide.

Cruising Guide to the Great Lakes, by Marjorie Cahn Brazer. Chicago: Contemporary Books, Inc., 1985; thorough, well-researched, eminently readable.

Pacific Boating Almanac. Ventura, California: Western Marine Enterprises; useful Pacific information, available from the publisher (Box Q, Ventura, 93002) or from selected chandleries.

The Practical Pilot, by Leonard Eyges. Camden, Maine: International Marine Publishing Company, 1989; a commonsense approach to coastal navigation.

FINDING YOUR WAY AROUND

American Automobile Association (AAA) Road Atlas: detailed, clear maps, travel tips, state, provincial, and national parks listings—everything you'll need; 8111 Gatehouse Road, Falls Church, VA 22047.

Charlie's Charts, by Charles and Margo Wood: three publications cover the West Coast from Mexico to Alaska; check your chandlery.

Baja Boater's Guides 1 and 2, by Jack Williams: a mixture of charts, text, and aerial photographs; check your chandlery.

The Waterway Guides: details routes, conditions, points of interest along the Intracoastal Waterway in New England, the Mid-Atlantic, Florida, and Gulf states; 6255 Barfield Road, Atlanta, GA 30328.

Weekly Trip Organizer					*Dates: from* _____ *to* _____			
Day	*Motoring*				*Sailing*			
	From	To	Via Routes	Miles	From	To	Miles	To See
		Total miles driven:				Total miles sailed:		

Estimated food expenses: _____ Estimated lodging expenses: _____

Estimated gas expenses: _____ Estimated other expenses: _____

ESTIMATED TOTAL EXPENSES: _____

Looking for a Few Good Gadgets

THE OREGO 5000 "HEAT PAL"

We sail in New England. The fall is clear and particularly beautiful here, but sometimes it gets nippy at night. A cabin heating stove is in order. Our Potter 19 isn't massive enough for a traditional potbellied stove (though that would be nice) but we finally found just the thing: the "Heat Pal."

The Heat Pal is about the size of a small wastebasket and it weighs about as much. About a papercupful of alcohol fuel is poured into a glass wool reservoir. If the stove is knocked over, you won't have a puddle of fire spreading across your cabin floor. The Heat Pal 5000 doesn't throw off a swelter of heat, nor will it ignite bedding, paper, or nearby combustibles. You can pick the stove up while it's running! The heated air flows *through* it.

This is a stove for taking the edge off a cold night (and maybe warming a pot of coffee on it in the process) . . . and it's safe. With all heaters of this sort, ventilation is absolutely vital lest your stove compete successfully against you for the oxygen in your cabin.

For this and other useful equipment, try E&B Discount Marine (800-533-5007) on the East Coast, or West Marine Products (800-538-0775) on the West Coast. Both offer catalogs.

THE NICRO-FICO SOLAR LO-VENT

The sun propels a tiny fan that pulls fresh air into your boat. All winter long this little fan changes the air in your cabin. Best of all, in *hot* weather, this fan doesn't provide a hurricane of cool air, but it *does* make a difference. This difference is noticeable if you remove the Solar Vent . . . uncomfortable becomes unbearable. We've used the Solar Vent in Lake Powell in Arizona, and in Florida—both in summer. This isn't a gimmick; it's a useful product.

OTHER GOOD STUFF

Downy Fabric Softener. Not a gadget, really, but useful on a small boat. Half a capful can turn a gallon of seawater into suitable bathing water that doesn't leave you feeling sticky later. It really works! Let a capful stand in a potty bowl filled with water overnight to sweeten the bowl—or scrub the cooler, sink, or head with it.

Liquid Paraffin. Beats kerosene lamp oils. *No* odor. Find a restaurant near you that has oil lamps on the tables and ask the manager to sell you a shampoo bottle-full. Makes oil lamps practical in small cabins.

Mateflex Matting. Its original version with diagonal hatching makes durable and attractive cockpit flooring. We use beige in a white hull. Allows sand and dirt to fall through and drain out the drain without grinding it underfoot into the flooring. Make a pattern, cut to shape, drop in. Rubber matting is too flexible. Mateflex is stiffer. Can work on cabin floor in lieu of carpeting. P.O. Box 538, 1712 Erie St., Utica, N.Y. 13503 (Phone 315-733-4600).

Cheap Rip-Stop Tarps. These can be cut and sewn into awnings, sailcovers, etc. Pass a line through the grommets on one end, pull into a tight loop, and gather it into a closed bunch. Hoist to masthead. Lines from free corners control set of this cheapo spinnaker. Satisfactory in light airs. Later, use as boomtent. Dragging your boat onto the beach? Spread down the tarp first, pull boat onto it. Now wave action won't gradually sand your bottom against the shore. When tarp wears out, use as dropcloth for next painting project.

Stainless Steel Broom/Mop Clip. It can be bolted to cabin ceiling. Flashlight can be clamped into it. Hang it near the hatchway. You can reach into the cabin to grab it immediately when needed. Doubles as a cabin light.

Beckson "Inspection Ports." These can be mounted on either side of your cockpit footwell to ventilate quarter berths. The company makes snap-in screens to keep the bugs out.

Weekly Trip Expense Record					Dates: from _____ to _____					
Day	Day's End Location	Total Gas	Total Tolls	Groc. & Pharm.	Total Bkfst.	Total Lunch	Total Dinner	Hotel or Camp	Total Misc.	Day's Total
Weekly Totals										
		Gas	Tolls	Groc.	Bkfst.	Lunch	Dinner	Lodging	Misc.	Week's Total

Index